School Counselor Consultation

♦

School Counselor Consultation

*Developing Skills for Working Effectively
with Parents, Teachers, and Other School Personnel*

♦

**Greg Brigman
Fran Mullis
Linda Webb
JoAnna White**

WILEY

John Wiley & Sons, Inc.

♦ Contents

◆ *List of Tables and Figures*

◆ *Foreword*

Before there were many counselors in the schools, teachers were asked to be teachers/counselors/consultants and to work on their own with students and parents who needed special attention. The concerns and interests of so many students and families were overwhelming, and there was a need for more guidance specialists.

When certified counselors were employed in large numbers during the 1970s, the popular idea was to provide students opportunities to meet face-to-face with their counselors in private sessions. However, high counselor-student ratios in almost every school made it impossible to provide extensive counseling services to students. Brief counseling and group counseling approaches were quickly considered practical methods.

Even more practical was the idea of a school counselor consulting with teachers, parents, and administrators about the needs and interests of students. Consulting put the counselor in the role of being an advocate, an educator, an ombudsman, and a group facilitator. School counselors became counselor/consultants.

It was about 30 years ago that consultation was first viewed as an actual practice of most counselors, even though it was seldom emphasized as a helping process or intervention during counselor education. It just seemed to come with the territory. There was no universally recognized definition, except that most agreed it involved a professional helping someone regarding a third person or group.

Consultation is an indirect approach in which a school counselor, functioning as a consultant, meets with a third party to talk about a student's interests and progress. This might include individual and group meetings with teachers, parents, and administrators. It could involve community health services. It might also, on occasion, consist of meeting with a student who is concerned about another student or group of students.

Early surveys showed that counselors did not differentiate counseling and consultation. It was assumed that the goals and communication skills of both were so similar that it was not necessary to distinguish one from the other. While there are many similarities, they are different and the most effective counselors know how to manage their skills accordingly.

Counseling has a rich, theoretical base, much of which has been drawn from schools of therapy and counseling psychology. Although most therapeutic methods must be modified for school settings, the theories and skills used in clinical counseling and psychotherapy provide concepts that define the counseling process. Consultation lacks a comparable theoretical foundation and is typically described in terms of consultant methods and skills.

One of the oldest approaches to consultation is the diagnostic-prescriptive method in which a consultant examines a consultee's situation and offers advice. For instance, a counselor/consultant may advise a teacher to talk with parents or perhaps meet with a student in an after-school conference. Sometimes, teachers are advised to work with students in a certain way so that they will be less disruptive or more involved in classroom activities. It's a common approach, but risky. Most people are skeptical about advice and prefer to find their own solutions.

The case consultation approach, as described in this book, focuses on a particular situation. The consultee is coached through a thinking process and then takes responsibility for implementing subsequent actions. Consultees are facilitated to talk about a case in a systematic way so that a plan of action can be constructed.

Sometimes people lack certain skills in their work that prevent them from being successful or from accomplishing more. Through training workshops, they might review or learn new skills and attitudes. Staff development and training workshops address knowledge and competencies. Training workshops provide opportunities to explore ideas and view matters from a different perspective. They can inspire people and help them gain more self-confidence and make commitments.

The authors of this book describe how you might work with teachers and parents in a workshop model that features warm-ups, timely information, and practice sessions. Examples of effective teacher skill-building programs are provided. For instance, teachers can be prepared to lead students in classroom meetings built around activities and discussions aimed at problem solving. Parent-teacher conferences require consultation skills.

Consultation is an effective use of a counselor's time. In addition to assisting people with problems or making decisions so that they can be better educators and helpers, consultation can play a significant part in developing a positive school climate.

Both counseling and consultation are viable interventions that help define the role and function of school counselors. This book is a guide for more effective consultation.

ROBERT D. MYRICK, PhD
Professor Emeritus
University of Florida

1

— ♦ —

Introduction to School Counselors as Consultants

— ♦ —

The importance of consultation has been discussed for years. In 1962, Gilbert Wrenn stressed its importance in his book *Counseling in a Changing World.* Faust (1968), in his now classic book for elementary school counselors, stated that consultation was more important than either group or individual counseling. Dinkmeyer and Caldwell (1970) recognized consultation as a key component of a developmental guidance program. Over the years, consultation as a counselor intervention has continued to receive support (Dustin & Ehly, 1992; Gysbers & Henderson, 2000; Paisley & McMahon, 2001; Wittmer, 2000). The National Standards of the American School Counselor Association (Campbell & Dahir, 1997) include consultation as one of four services critical to the successful implementation of a comprehensive developmental school guidance and counseling program.

Writers such as Dinkmeyer, Carlson, and Dinkmeyer (2000) and Myrick (2003) encourage school counselors to consult with adults, because children and adolescents are often powerless to make changes; therefore, it is more useful to work with the significant adults in their lives. Consultation is also time efficient. The counselor can teach the consultee skills that may be applied in similar situations. Thus, more children and adolescents can be reached through consultation than through individual or small group counseling.

The effective consultant, as described by Dougherty (2000), has the following attributes:

1

1. A personal and professional growth orientation
2. Knowledge of consultation and human behavior
3. Consulting skills

We have added a fourth attribute:

4. A multicultural and diversity perspective

PERSONAL AND PROFESSIONAL GROWTH ORIENTATION

An orientation toward personal growth is not something that can be taught in graduate school, but it is an attitude toward life that can be encouraged. Any activity that is new or different could be considered a growth activity, whether cognitive, physical, emotional, or spiritual. Professional growth means participating in activities that specifically lead to being a more effective consultant, and it could include academic courses, workshops, professional reading, and supervised practice.

To be effective, the school counselor must have a growth orientation. If we expect students, teachers, and administrators to make changes in their lives, we must also be willing to grow and change. The number of topics about which counselors as consultants must be knowledgeable increases each year. All of these topics cannot possibly be taught within a one-quarter or one-semester consultation course. If counselors are to remain competent in their field, professional growth activities are critical.

KNOWLEDGE OF CONSULTATION AND HUMAN BEHAVIOR

Many of the courses required for a master's degree in school counseling, such as theories of learning and theories of behavior change, help the consultant gain knowledge of human behavior. Although other courses in a school counseling program might touch on consultation, the most effective way to gain a knowledge of consultation is to complete specific training in that area.

CONSULTING SKILLS

Preparing to become effective consultants in the school includes knowledge of:

- Consultation models/theory
- Human development
- Available resources for parents[1] and teachers
- A wide range of student issues/concerns

Preparation also includes using effective helping skills and ethical guidelines to support consultative skills in facilitating:

- The individual case consultative process (with parents, teachers, and administrators)
- Parenting group meetings
- Teacher and parent workshops
- Team meetings

A MULTICULTURAL AND DIVERSITY PERSPECTIVE

The *American School Counselor Association (ASCA) Ethical Standards for School Counselors* (2004) states that school counselors must recognize that differences in clients relating to age, gender, race, religion, sexual orientation, socioeconomic, ethnic backgrounds and other differences may require specific training to ensure competent services. This is true with regard to consultation as well as to counseling. Effective school counselors maintain a multicultural or diversity perspective in all of their interactions with students, parents, teachers, other school personnel, and community resources.

All counseling (and by extension, all consultation) is multicultural, "because all individuals are members of many cultures in which different values are required" (Herring, 1997, p. 7). Herring distinguishes between the terms *multicultural* and *diversity*. Multicultural "refers to five major cultural groups in the United States and its territories: African/Black, Asian, Caucasian/European, Hispanic/Latino, and Native American. . . ." (p. 6). Diversity pertains to characteristics other than culture, such as age, gender, race, religion or spiritual identification, sexual orientation, socioeconomic class, and place of residence, such as urban, suburban, or rural. The Preamble of the *ASCA Code of Ethics* adds marital status to the aforementioned list and we believe that disabilities and learning styles are other differences that school counselors must be attuned to, especially when

---

[1] The word *parent* or *parents* will be used to denote parents, guardians, or any other person who has legal responsibility for a child.

consulting with teachers about a student's academic performance. School counselors must be mindful that all of the above differences may affect how parents, teachers, and others perceive consultation in general and the interventions suggested in particular.

It is not the purpose of this book to describe the characteristics of specific multicultural populations or to discuss all of the areas of diversity listed earlier. There are many good books and journals available to help the school counselor or school counselor-in-training acquire knowledge and skills in these areas (e.g., Herring, 1997; Sue & Sue, 2003; and the *Journal of Multicultural Counseling and Development* published by the American Counseling Association). We provide the following suggestions to assist school counselors in maintaining a multicultural and diversity perspective in their work with students, parents, teachers, other school personnel, and community resources:

- Although it is helpful to understand the typical characteristics of different multicultural groups, it is important to realize that there are more differences *within* groups than there are *between* groups (Sue & Sue, 2003). Also, if you are consulting with someone from a different country, it is useful to determine their level of acculturation.

- Remember that even though some parents' values may be very different from your values, all parents (with some exceptions, perhaps) love their children and want the best for them. Acknowledging this love and letting parents know that you care about their child and want the child to be successful goes far in getting and keeping the parents' cooperation and assistance.

- Keep in mind that every consultee has a personal history that is unique and that influences his or her belief system (LaFromboise et al., 1996, as cited in Baker & Gerler, 2004). Taking time to learn about consultees' belief systems not only will help establish rapport, but also will help you suggest interventions that are compatible with their beliefs. Compatible interventions are more likely to be implemented. Suggestions for ascertaining this information are provided in later chapters.

- When suggesting interventions, it is helpful to consider possible consequences regarding other family and community members (LaFromboise et al., 1996, as cited in Baker & Gerler, 2004; Mullis & Edwards, 2001). For example, if a student's parents decide that they will not insist that the student follow the family tradition of becoming a medical doctor, help them reflect on the reactions of other family members, such as grandparents, and how they will manage those reactions.

- You also have a personal history that shapes your belief system. Take time to examine your values and beliefs. If culturally laden values and beliefs are unexamined, they are often thought to be "correct," rather than just one way of looking at issues. After identifying your values, ask yourself how you came to have these values and if these values could conflict with the values of others.

Acquiring this knowledge and these skills might seem difficult and time consuming. However, it is worth the work required to become a skilled and effective consultant because of the rewards gained from assisting children through consultation with the important adults in their lives.

WHY CONSULT?

There are a variety of reasons why school counselors must become effective consultants in order to meet the needs of students:

- Consultation is a holistic approach to understanding and assisting students with academic, personal/social, and career issues and decisions.
- Consultation reaches the most students through the most effective use of the counselor's time.
- Consultation experiences with teachers, parents, and administrators help to develop a positive school climate.
- Consultation with teachers, parents, and administrators empowers significant adults in the lives of the students to develop effective strategies for parenting and teaching.
- Consultation enables the school counselor to develop trusting relationships with teachers, administrators, and parents.
- Consultation is one important approach through which school counselors can make their role clear to parents and school personnel.
- Consultation provides the school counselor with an opportunity to advocate for the rights of children and adolescents.
- Consultation is the most effective way to interact with community members and referral sources that are concerned about the education of children and teens.

Whether you are a graduate student training to become a school counselor, a new school counselor just setting up your program, or an experienced counselor seeking new ideas to expand or simplify your consultation process, we hope you find this book helpful.

The authors have been practicing school counselors and are now counselor educators. Because of our combined 38 years of experience as school counselors and our combined 53 years of experience supervising school counselor interns, we recognized the need for a practical, skills-based text to help the consultation process operate more effectively. We hope to reduce some of the anxieties you may have in working with the various stakeholders in an educational setting.

Chapter 1 introduces you to the importance of consultation in schools, discusses attributes of the effective consultant, and presents reasons for becoming an effective consultant. Chapter 1, describes several theoretical models (Adlerian, cognitive behavioral, multimodal, reality therapy, and solution focused) that the authors believe are useful in school consultation. They also describe several consultation models (behavioral, mental health, and organizational), as well as the case consultation model used in this book.

The ethical issues most germane to the consultation process are discussed in Chapter 3, including the particular concerns surrounding confidentiality when consulting about minors in the school setting. Chapter 4 provides a detailed description of the five-step case consultation model used by the authors. Issues that often must be addressed by school counselors are presented in Chapter 5. Suggestions about teaching teachers how to refer students to counselors, as well as what to tell teachers and parents to tell students about seeing the counselor are given. Consultee resistance is also addressed. Chapter 6 provides information about how to structure workshops for teachers and parents. Examples of packaged programs that are useful are also offered.

Collaboration is a skill that school counselors as consultants must develop. Parent-teacher-counselor, student-teacher-counselor, and teacher team consultation is addressed in Chapter 7. Recommendations for interventions are also provided. Chapter 8 proposes the use of classroom meetings as a way to create a schoolwide climate of cooperation. Chapter 9 offers examples of ways counselors can consult with administrators to develop schoolwide plans. Crisis intervention plans and discipline plans are presented. Chapter 10 suggests ways, such as using community task forces and speaker's bureaus, to involve the community in the school.

There are four appendices: The first provides an overview of Adlerian theory, the second contains the ASCA Ethical Standards, and the third appendix contains the American Counseling Association (ACA) Code of

Ethics. The fourth appendix is a guide to using this text to build consultation skills. It may be used by instructors who teach a class on consultation to school counselors-in-training, but also will be useful to practicing school counselors who want to enhance their consultation skills. School counselors-in-training are encouraged to read this appendix because it provides an overview of the goals for this text, as well as a self-assessment of consultation knowledge and skills. Following the reference list is an annotated bibliography that lists useful books about Adlerian theory, ethics, and consultation.

This book provides a practical model for school counselors to follow in their consultation sessions. It is designed to serve as a guide; school counselors will develop their own style for interaction on behalf of students. Building this type of program is a process; it cannot be done all at once. To build success into your plan, you must not take on too much the first year.

Consultation can be one of the most time-effective and beneficial services that school counselors provide. We encourage all school counselors to get involved in the consultation process and experience the positive results.

2

— ♦ —

A School-Based Approach to Consultation: Supporting Models and Theories

— ♦ —

CONSULTATION IN SCHOOLS

To be successful in the consultant role, school counselors must have a theoretical base and models from which to operate. Theory provides a basis for understanding what helps people change their attitudes, skills, behaviors, and expectations (West & Idol, 1987). Models provide a conceptual framework for practice (Kratochwill & Bergan, 1990). A number of school consultation models are discussed in the professional literature (Brack, Jones, Smith, White, & Brack, 1993; Dustin & Ehly, 1992; Erchul & Conoley, 1991; Fall, 1995; Kern & Mullis, 1993; Keys, Bemak, Carpenter, & King-Sears, 1998; Otwell & Mullis, 1997; West & Idol, 1993; White & Mullis, 1998). As with all models of consultation, these use problem-solving approaches to help consultees with school-related concerns and help them be more effective with similar problems in the future (Dougherty, 2000).

The approach to consultation in the schools presented in this text is supported by theory while drawing on established models to create a framework that will meet the needs of school counselors working as consultants. This approach is also aligned with implementation of the National Standards of the American School Counselor Association (Campbell & Dahir, 1997) including consultation as one of the services critical to successful implementation of comprehensive developmental school guidance and counseling program.

9

THEORETICAL APPROACH

An integration of theory is used to support the consultation model we have developed for school use. We have used a combination of Adlerian, cognitive behavioral, and behavioral lenses to view the consultative relationship and problem-solving process. The consultation model presented in the text is also compatible with reality therapy and solution-focused approaches. While we believe having a theoretical approach is essential, no particular theory is a requirement for using the model. The model itself provides structure; the lens can reflect the consultant's own personal integration of theory.

Of the multitude of theoretical approaches to counseling and structuring consultation, we have found several to be most useful. Adlerian theory provides a sound educational premise for use with both students and adults (White, Mullis, Earley, & Brigman, 1995). Adlerian theory fits what we do in schools because it is future oriented, collaborative, and realistic. It emphasizes social interest and the importance of contributing to society.

Key principles of Adlerian theory as applied to consultation include:

- Equality between the consultant and the consultee
- Encouragement
- Respect
- The mistaken goals of behavior
- Logical consequences
- Family atmosphere
- Faith in the client (child) and consultee (parent, teacher, administrator)

The emphasis is on offering education and training to parents and teachers and the sharing of information and ideas. Teachers trained in Adlerian theory strive for democratic classrooms. They can identify mistaken goals of behavior in students. They use encouragement rather than praise and logical consequences instead of punishment.

Key principles and constructs from Adler's theory (Adler, 1927/1971) have provided the framework for concepts adapted for use in schools by Dinkmeyer and Carlson (1973) and Dinkmeyer, Pew, and Dinkmeyer (1979). We have found these applied Adlerian concepts to be understandable and based on common sense. When asking parents and teachers to try a new way of doing things at school or at home, the results will be more successful if your approach is practical. Adlerian materials provide how-to solutions for classroom or home situations. Additional information about Adlerian theory is found in Appendix A.

Cognitive behavioral (Beck, 1976) and behavioral techniques are also helpful in providing structure for intervention planning. They provide clear, measurable, action-oriented approaches to helping change behavior. A problem-solving sequence with baseline data and measurable student outcomes lends itself well to the data-driven accountability of today's programs.

School counselors as consultants can help teachers and parents understand the principles involved in encouraging responsible pro-social student behaviors that increase student success. They can help teachers examine their own cognitive framework in relation to the students they teach, opening the door for improved student outcomes. Consultants can facilitate the development of mutually agreed on intervention involving behavior contracts and management plans.

The multimodal approach of behavioral therapy developed by Lazarus (1981) was adapted by Keat (1990) for use with children and adolescents. His HELPING acronym (see Table 2.1) represents a holistic and systemic approach which helps give counselors and teachers/parents a broader view of how the child or adolescent is functioning. By understanding the overall functioning of the student, counselors, teachers, and parents can improve their chances of developing a successful plan of action.

Especially relevant to consultation is the guidance portion of the HELPING model. At both the counselor/teacher/parent level and the teacher/parent/student level, the notion of guidance of actions, behavior, and consequences is useful. Guidance emphasizes modeling, teaching, self-monitoring, contracting, and environmental restructuring.

The counselor uses each of these strategies while working with the teacher/parent and also encourages the teacher/parent to use this approach when working with the student.

Table 2.1   The HELPING Model

H = Health
E = Emotions
L = Learning
P = Personal relationships
I = Imagery
N = Needs to know
G = Guidance

Reality Therapy (Glasser, 2000) emphasizes the notion of future-oriented behavior and looking for productive ways for people to achieve their goals. Some of the key principles of Reality Therapy that this consultation model finds compatible are the importance of building a good relationship, helping the client examine current behavior and evaluate if it is helpful or not, brainstorming alternatives, committing to new plan, and evaluating results without punishment or excuses, and, finally, the importance of not getting discouraged or giving up.

The solution-focused approach (de Shazer, 1988) emphasizes looking for strengths, assets, and past successes to build on for planning future successful actions. Encouraging teachers and parents to explore strengths and assets of students who are having problems encourages them to shift their perception of the student and the situation and become more hopeful. An emphasis on looking for signs of even very small improvement is a helpful perspective that reinforces positive effort and builds confidence. This approach is also future oriented with most of the time spent focused on the solution rather than the problem. These components of the solution-focused approach are embedded in this consultation model. A consultative model that provides school counselors with a logical framework that facilitates the problem-solving process is discussed next.

MODELS OF CONSULTATION

Models of consultation have been organized in different ways. One approach has been to consider the primary focus of the consultation. Dougherty (2000) described behavioral, mental health, and organizational models.

The primary focus of *behavioral consultation* (Bergan, 1977) is to foster specific changes in the frequency of behaviors in the client, consultee, or client system. The process involves clearly defined steps geared toward problem identification, analysis, plan implementation, and plan evaluation. The behavioral model helps provide a structural framework for school counselors as they provide a systematic problem-solving process to assist teachers and parents with students.

Bergan and Kratochwill (1990) see the role of the behavioral consultant as facilitating this process of evaluation and planning, including the development of interventions that can be evaluated for their effectiveness. As school counselors strive to project a clear purpose/mission, measurable outcomes involving interventions become important. Behavioral approaches to consultation have been used in schools and other environments that are mainly under the control of caretakers with the assumption that changing the environment will produce behavioral changes (Conoley & Conoley, 1992). Over the years, behavioral consultation application has progressed to include a more cognitive component addressing internal components that may affect behavior as well (Kratochwill, Sladeezek, & Plunge, 1995).

Mental health consultation, developed by Gerald Caplan (1970), seeks to help the consultee understand client interactions that may stem from lack of skills, knowledge, self-esteem, or professional objectivity. The goal of the consultation is to help the consultee become more effective professionally by providing knowledge, teaching skills, or facilitating a change in self-esteem or professional objectivity.

Dougherty (2000) considers the Adlerian approach a form of mental health consultation with its emphasis on education and training for parents and teachers and has described the process. The consultant begins by gathering information on the case prior to meeting with the teacher/parent. The consultant then asks the teacher/parent to tell his or her story to learn more about the relationship and teacher's/parent's feelings to be able to pinpoint the goal of the student's behavior. The consultant may also observe the student in the classroom. Appropriate agreed on interventions can then be discussed. Short-term behavioral goals are the focus.

White and Mullis (1998) have also described an Adlerian approach involving four stages, each essential in order to move on to the next:

1. A respectful, encouraging relationship must first be developed to promote a sense of working together.
2. Problems are then identified and there is agreement as to what to work on.
3. An exploration of the child's functioning within the social contexts of home and school, sibling and peer relationships, as well as an exploration of strengths and weaknesses provide a better understanding of what might help.
4. Finally, the consultant and consultee work together to formulate a plan built on encouragement and cooperation.

During this process, the consultant is teaching the parent or teacher concepts that may help them better understand their child or student such as goals of misbehavior, use of encouragement, and use of logical consequences.

The focus of *organizational consultation* is to enhance the overall effectiveness of the organization. The client system is the organization itself or some part of it. Interventions are designed that help the organization's members become more satisfied and productive, resulting in a change in the system of the organization. Dougherty (2000) suggests that the differences between the major consultative models have become less distinct with more similarities than differences. All consultation occurs within an organization, affects the well-being of the consultee and client system, and works toward change. When consultees, clients, or client systems respond positively to consultation, their behaviors change.

ANOTHER APPROACH TO ORGANIZATION OF MODELS

Another approach to organizing models of consultation has been to consider the types of interactions among the participants of the consultation (Keys et al., 1998) including triadic-dependent, collaborative-dependent, or collaborative-independent. A triadic-dependent interaction involves a three-person relationship with the consultant indirectly bringing about change in the client or student through direct service with the consultee, usually the parent or teacher. In this model, the consultee is seeking assistance from the consultant seen as the expert providing recommendations.

In a collaborative-dependent model, the consultant facilitates the problem-solving process while establishing mutual goals and agreed on interventions with the consultee who then delivers the interventions. This would still be a triadic interaction however; both the consultant and consultee would be contributing expertise and knowledge in the problem-solving process with the consultant providing education about problem solving. This process allows for future problem solving and is consistent with a developmental school counseling approach.

Keys et al. (1998) and others (Idol, Nevin, & Paolucci-Witcomb, 1994; West & Idol, 1993) have also described models of collaborative consultation that provide a framework for allowing groups of people with diverse expertise to generate creative solutions to mutually defined problems (Idol et al., 1994). This type of consultation model moves away from the triadic models and toward a team approach with the consultant facilitating the process as well as contributing expertise as one of its members. It involves the sharing of information, formation of goals and objectives, intervention planning, and outcome evaluation. Counselors as consultants in schools frequently facilitate teams of professionals planning interventions for more effective student outcomes. Keys et al. refers to this model as a collaborative-independent model.

It is important to note that even though the terms consultation and collaboration are often used interchangeably, they are somewhat different. *Consultation* is a triadic process through which the counselor assists the consultee in his or her relationship with someone else. For example, the school counselor/consultant consults with a teacher about a child's classroom behavior.

Collaboration, in the truest sense, is a process that takes consultation a step further (Myrick, 2003). When collaborating, the consultant takes at least partial responsibility for implementing the plan made through consultation. For example, the school counselor who has consulted with a teacher about student behavior might also work directly with the student.

MODELS AND THEORY CENTRAL TO THIS APPROACH

Consultation for counselors who work primarily with children and adolescents in schools typically involves assisting teachers with individual students and groups of students who have developmental as well as special needs. In addition, it involves providing resources and education to parents and teachers through workshops and parent education classes, interpreting student information, and consulting with teams of professionals (Glosoff & Koprowicz, 1990; White et al., 1995).

The model for consultation in the schools presented in this text is an integrated approach. Education and training to increase the effectiveness of the consultee are part of this approach along with a collaborative model for working with a team of professionals.

The types of interactions school counselors have with consultees vary based on the nature of the consultation. When working with an individual teacher, parent, or administrator, our approach reflects a collaborative-dependent relationship stressing mutual goals and agreed on interventions to be delivered by the consultee. The approach incorporates various concepts including consultant-consultee equity, building on strengths and past successes, encouragement, collaborative problem solving, and faith in the client and consultee. Within this context, the consultant facilitates movement through a series of steps described shortly, and toward developing a plan that will result in changed client/student behavior.

As school counselors/consultants work with teams of professionals the relationship follows a more collaborative independent model with the counselor facilitating the process as well as contributing expertise as one of its members. The principles noted previously and the case consultation model that follows are used as a guide for facilitating the process.

CASE CONSULTATION MODEL

The five steps outlined in Table 2.2 describe the basic model followed throughout this book. More detail will be provided in Chapter 4 regarding the five-step model, as well as information related specifically to consultation with parents, teachers, administrators, and teams of professionals. A "before, during, and after the consultation" format is used in discussing the model.

TEACHING/WORKSHOP MODEL

Group and workshop facilitation are also part of the school counselor's consultative role. In this relationship, the consultant is generally regarded as having expertise on a topic and facilitates the learning process for participants. The teaching/workshop model provides opportunities to educate parents and teachers about behavior and ways to effectively encourage and redirect students.

The following format provides consultants with a framework with which to facilitate learning. It allows for the inclusion of a wide variety of activities while keeping participants engaged as they integrate and apply what they are learning. The model is described in detail in Chapter 6.

1. *Warm-up:* Introduce the topic/engage the participants.
2. *Ask before telling:* Participants are asked to share some of their thoughts before information is presented.

Table 2.2 Case Consultation Model

Before the Consultation
  Step I Prepare for the consultation.

During the Consultation
  Step II   Define the process and develop the relationship.
  Step III Present and gather information about the child.
  Step IV Formulate intervention strategies and plan for implementation and follow-up.

After the Consultation
  Step V   Follow-up of consultation.

3. *Introduction of information and skills:* The consultant shares expertise on topic/teaches and demonstrates any new skills to be learned.

4. *Personalize and practice:* Participants are asked to think, write, and share experiences related to topic and are given a chance to practice any new skills.

5. *Process and summarize:* Participants reflect on workshop experience and how they will use what they have learned.

6. *Evaluate:* Feedback regarding targeted outcomes.

The approaches described in this chapter draw from behavioral and mental health models supported by concepts of Adlerian, cognitive behavioral, and behavioral theories and are compatible with Realty Therapy and solution-focused approaches. The nature of the consultant's relationship with the consultee depends on the type of consultative experience; whether it is case consultation or educational. It is a brief approach that makes sense for schools. We encourage you to make it part of your approach.

3

— ♦ —

Ethical Issues in Consultation

— ♦ —

Many school counselors belong to the American School Counselor Association (ASCA) and to the American Counseling Association (ACA), both of which have codes of ethics. Although the *ASCA Ethical Standards* (2004; see Appendix B) does not specifically address the issue of counselor as consultant, the *ACA Code of Ethics* (1995; see Appendix C) includes standards that pertain to consultation. School counselors are responsible for acting in accordance with the ethical code(s) of the professional organization(s) to which they belong. Ethical issues are related to various characteristics of the consultation relationship, which are shown below:

- Tripartite (consultant-consultee-client)
- Nonsupervisory
- Voluntary
- Temporary
- Work-related

TRIPARTITE RELATIONSHIP

School counselors often consult with teachers, parents, and others about students. The student is the client and does not usually participate in the consultation; however, the focus is on the student and this is what makes consultation a tripartite relationship. *Confidentiality* is the primary ethical concern that arises from this type of relationship and involves:

- Information about the student (client)
- Information about the consultee

Both the ASCA and ACA ethical codes clearly state that information obtained in the counseling relationship is to be held in confidence unless permission to disclose that information is given or unless that information is exempt from confidentiality.

Section A.2(b and c) of the *ASCA Ethical Standards* addresses this aspect of confidentiality:

> b. The professional school counselor keeps information confidential unless disclosure is required to prevent clear and imminent danger to the student or others or when legal requirements demand that confidential information be revealed. Counselors will consult with appropriate professionals when in doubt as to the validity of an exception, and
>
> c. In absence of state legislation expressly forbidding disclosure, considers the ethical responsibility to provide information to an identified third party who, by his/her relationship with the student, is at a high risk of contracting a disease that is commonly known to be communicable and fatal. Disclosure requires satisfaction of all of the following conditions:
> - Student identifies partner or the partner is highly identifiable
> - Counselor recommends the student notify partner and refrain from further high-risk behavior
> - Student refuses
> - Counselor informs the student of the intent to notify the partner
> - Counselor seeks legal consultation as to the legalities of informing the partner

INFORMATION ABOUT THE STUDENT (CLIENT)

The *ASCA Ethical Standards* do not discuss confidentiality specifically with regard to consultation; however, both the *ASCA Ethical Standards* and the *ACA Code of Ethics* do mention sharing information with other agencies/persons in the section of the code addressing confidentiality. Because confidentiality is essential for safeguarding the welfare of the consultee and the student, it should be strictly observed in the consulting relationship. If a teacher or parent consults with you about a student, information about that student should be kept in confidence, just as it would be if you were working directly with the student. Giving information about the student to the principal or to others is a breach of confidentiality. It is also a breach of confidentiality to inform others that the teacher or parent consulted with you or to share information that they provided about themselves, unless given permission to do so.

If parents give you information about their child, it is a good idea to ask permission to share that information with the teacher or other adults who work with that child so that they can be more effective. For example, a parent might tell you that a divorce is being discussed at home. Telling the student's teacher could be very helpful, and often the parent is relieved to have the information shared—especially if you give only general information and keep the details to yourself. If the parents do not give you permission to share information, then it would be unethical to do so.

Many times, parents and teachers who consult with you also want you to counsel with their child or student. Counseling with a student who is referred by someone else complicates not only the counseling process, but also confidentiality issues. When parents or teachers refer someone to the counselor, they frequently believe they have a right to know what is discussed in the counseling session and are interested in the child's welfare. Although parents of a minor child have a legal right to know what occurs during counseling, counselors can be most effective with students if the concerns discussed are kept confidential. The *ASCA Ethical Standards* (B.2 Parents/Guardians and Confidentiality) addresses this issue. Counselors must explain to the parents the importance of confidentiality when counseling their child. Counselors can tell parents something like the following: "I know that you are interested in everything your son has to say to me. But for me to work most effectively with him, it is helpful if what we talk about is just between the two of us. Of course, if there is something that could be harmful to him, I will discuss that with you. Otherwise, I would like to be able to offer him confidentiality and talk with you about some things you might do at home to be helpful."

When teachers are the referring agents, counselors also can explain the importance of confidentiality to the counseling process. In addition, counselors can write the teacher a note after each counseling session, briefly describing how counseling is proceeding (Carlson, 1990). For example, the counselor could thank the teacher for sending the student to the counseling office and say that he or she and the student are getting to know one another, or that he or she believes some progress is being made without going into detail. The *ASCA Ethical Standards* (C.2.b Sharing Information with Other Professionals) states that "The professional school counselor provides professional personnel with accurate, objective, concise, and meaningful data necessary to adequately evaluate, counsel, and assist the student." Offering helpful, but general information often satisfies the referring person's interest in the student without harming the counseling relationship by breaching confidentiality.

Some students do not mind if you discuss their concerns with their parents or teachers. When a student has been referred by a parent or teacher, at the end of the counseling session the counselor can ask the student if it would be all right to talk with the adult about the student's concerns. If the student has been referred by a teacher because he or she is no longer consistently completing homework, for example, the counselor might find out that the child's uncle, aunt, and their three children have moved into the child's home temporarily and there is not a quiet place to do homework. In this case, the counselor might say, "I know your teacher is concerned about you, wonders about the reason you are not completing homework and will probably ask me about our session. What would you like for me to tell her?" This provides the student an opportunity to have input into what is told and also alerts him or her that some information might be shared. The counselor could also ask the student if he or she would like to talk with the teacher about the reason homework is not being completed, or suggest something that the counselor could say to the teacher. In the previous example, the counselor might say, "Would it be okay if I told your teacher that you have had some changes at your home that make it difficult for you to have a quiet place to study?" If the child objects to sharing any information, it would be most helpful to the counseling relationship to keep the information confidential. The same steps can be taken if the parent is the referring person.

However, Section A. 2 (b and c) of the *ASCA Ethical Standards* states that there are times when information is exempt from confidentiality requirements. For example, if the counselor learned that it was suspected that a student was being abused, as a mandated reporter, the counselor must report this to the proper authorities. The counselor would also need to act on information that a student was threatening to harm him or herself or another person.

Counselors may be subpoenaed to appear in court. Unless school counselors in your state have *privileged communication,* counselors must disclose information in a court of law. (It is important to check the laws in your state regarding privileged communication for school counselors. Sometimes, even if privilege is granted, it pertains only to specific areas.

Laws vary widely from state to state.) If you believe that it would be harmful to the consultee or counselee to disclose information in court, you can request that the information be given to the judge in private. The judge then decides if the information must be disclosed in open court (*ASCA Ethical Standards*, A.2.d).

INFORMATION ABOUT THE CONSULTEE

The consultee should be informed regarding confidentiality and reminded about these limits throughout the consultative process. One explanation for the resistance of some teachers to consult with you about problems in the classroom is that teachers are concerned that their performance evaluations will be adversely affected if the administration learns that they are having difficulty with students.

Teachers and other consultees should be told if a list is being kept of those seeking consultation. They should know who has access to that list and how the list is being used. To reduce teacher resistance to consultation, you should make certain that consultation information is safeguarded and is not being used inappropriately by yourself or others. For instance, you often must keep track of the number of teacher consultations you engage in for your own performance evaluation. Turning in a list of teacher names rather than simply a number would be a breach of confidentiality, regardless of how that list was used by the person receiving it.

In addition, information received in data collections, such as needs assessments and other surveys, should be kept confidential to ensure the integrity of the data. Survey participants may not provide accurate information about needs if they are concerned about the use that will be made of the data. Teachers may hesitate to admit the need for classroom management techniques if they fear that the administration will see the survey and make negative judgments about their competence. Participants should be informed prior to data collection about how the information will be shared and used. Again, teacher fears can be allayed if the information is aggregated and only numbers, not names, are reported.

NONSUPERVISORY RELATIONSHIP

Consultation, especially with teachers, is a peer relationship. To be effective as a consultant, you should not have a supervisory role or be perceived

as someone who will report the nature of the consultation to the consultee's supervisor. Resistance to consultation can be greatly reduced if you
explain your role as a consultant in a way that emphasizes the egalitarian
nature of the relationship.

VOLUNTARY AND TEMPORARY RELATIONSHIP

The consultation relationship is voluntary and temporary because it is a relationship between peers. It also encourages consultee self-reliance.

Sections D.2.c and D.2.d of the *ACA Ethical Standards* addresses these
aspects of consultation:

> c. Understanding with Clients. When providing consultation, counselors at-
> tempt to develop with their clients a clear understanding of problem defini-
> tion, goals for change, and predicted consequences of interventions selected.
> d. Consultant Goals. The consulting relationship is one in which client
> adaptability and growth toward self-direction are consistently encouraged
> and cultivated.

VOLUNTARY AND TEMPORARY

Consultants do not attempt to force the consultee to go along with their
analysis of the problem or with suggested strategies for change. The consultee is an equal in the relationship and has the option not only of participating or not participating in consultation, but also of defining the
problem and selecting intervention strategies. As a consultant, it is appropriate to provide a rationale for your point of view regarding a student,
but the consultee is the person who must interact with the student and a
strategy with which he or she does not agree will not be used in a way to
guarantee failure.

Consultee self-direction is the principle objective of the standard just
discussed (*ACA Standards,* D.2.d). To encourage self-direction or freedom
of choice for the consultee, you may (and often *should*) offer suggestions,
but you must refrain from making decisions for the consultee and creating
dependency. The main purpose of providing consultation in the schools is
to help the consultee function more effectively and independently by providing alternative ways of viewing behavior and by offering interventions
that are not currently in the consultee's repertoire. By safeguarding the

voluntary and temporary nature of the consultation relationship and by encouraging consultee decision making about goals and interventions, you avoid fostering an ongoing, dependent relationship.

ENCOURAGES CONSULTEE SELF-RELIANCE

A primary rationale for providing consultation is that it is time-efficient. By working with teachers and parents, you can indirectly affect more students than you could by working directly with the students. Teachers often have 20 or more students in their classrooms. Assisting them with one student frequently offers insights about other students, as well as interventions that can be used with other students in their classrooms. The same efficiency holds true with parents if they have more than one child. Keeping teachers and parents dependent on you (although ego-boosting) is not a good use of your time. Remembering that the relationship is temporary can help you be efficient with your time. Although the consultee may end the relationship at any point regardless of problem status, once the problem has been resolved, the consultation relationship is automatically ended.

Informed consent is related to these and other aspects of the consultation relationship. Consultees need to be informed about the process and goals of consultation, its voluntary nature, the consultees' freedom of choice in following or not following the consultant's suggestions, and issues of confidentiality before they decide whether to participate in consultation. Although informed consent is an ongoing process, you may address these issues with groups of teachers, parents, or administrators and then review the issues at the beginning of individual consultation sessions. As consultation proceeds, informed consent issues may need to be discussed again.

Providing information about what consultation is and what you do in providing consultation can also help lessen resistance. When discussing your consultation role with others, you need to emphasize that the focus is on the client (the student) and not on the consultee, and that the purpose of consultation is to assist, not judge, the consultee.

WORK-RELATED RELATIONSHIP

Focus the consultation relationship on work-related problems, rather than on the personal problems of the consultee. By maintaining a work-related orientation, you avoid entering into a dual relationship with the consultee. Both the ASCA and ACA ethical codes address dual relationships. The *ASCA Ethical Standards* (A.4) states the following regarding dual relationships:

> The professional school counselor avoids dual relationships that might impair his or her objectivity and increase the risk of harm to the student (e.g., counseling one's family members, close friends, or associates). If a dual relationship is unavoidable, the counselor is responsible for taking action to eliminate or reduce the potential for harm. Such safeguards might include informed consent, consultation, supervision, and documentation.

It is difficult to adhere to a clear distinction between consultation and counseling, because school counselors are, after all, counselors, and it is a counselor's nature to believe it is helpful to work on personal issues. Also, personal concerns such as competency or control issues often arise when parents or teachers are having a problem with a child that results in a consultation with the counselor. These concerns must be attended to in order to encourage consultee self-reliance.

However, if the consultee's personal problems become the central concern, then consultation has become counseling and a dual relationship results. To avoid duality, you can refer the consultee to another counselor to work on personal issues. At the very least, you should inform the consultee that the focus of the relationship has shifted from a consulting orientation to a counseling orientation. In keeping with the standards of voluntary participation and informed consent, the consultee can decide to move into a counseling relationship or to return to the consultation relationship. If you do not call attention to the shift in focus, however, consultees may reveal personal information that they later regret. This could result in the consultee feeling uncomfortable and avoiding any type of relationship with you in the future. If this happens, you lose the opportunity to work indirectly with students in that classroom, or with that parent's child.

OTHER ETHICAL ISSUES

Other issues of an ethical nature specifically related to consultation are the following:

- Working with other professionals
- Competence
- Values
- Fees for services

WORKING WITH OTHER PROFESSIONALS

Sometimes it is necessary for the counselor to make referrals to a resource outside the school. According to the *ASCA Ethical Standards* (A.5) and the *ACA Code of Ethics* (A.11.b) counselors must make referrals when necessary or appropriate. The *ASCA Ethical Standards* (A.5) state:

> The professional school counselor makes referrals when necessary or appropriate to outside resources. Appropriate referral may necessitate informing both parents/guardians and students of applicable resources and making proper plans for transitions with minimal interruption of services. Students retain the right to discontinue the counseling relationship at any time. Counselees retain the right to discontinue the counseling relationship at any time.

If the school counselor continues to work with the student or family who has been referred by him or her to an outside resource, or if the counselor is asked to work with a student who is seeing a counselor or another mental health professional outside of the school, then both the ASCA and ACA Codes of Ethics are clear about the school counselor's responsibility to contact the other professional.

Section C.2.c of the *ASCA Ethical Standards* and section A.4 and C.6.c of the *ACA Ethical Standards* address these aspects of consultation. The *ASCA Ethical Standards* state:

> If a student is receiving services from another counselor or other mental health professional, the counselor, with student and/or parent/guardian consent, will inform the other professional and develop clear agreements to avoid confusion and conflict for the student.

The parent or guardian must give consent for a minor child. The school counselor as well as the outside mental health professional must have written consent to speak to each other about the student. When talking with the other professional, the school counselor must provide "accurate, objective, concise, and meaningful data" (*ASCA Ethical Standards,* C.2.b). It is most helpful to talk with the outside professional rather than simply ending school counseling services to students if they are engaged in therapy outside the school. It also is important to talk with the other professional to decide what school counseling services would be in the student's best interest. It is possible that individual counseling sessions with the student could be ended, but group counseling or occasionally touching base with the student might provide needed support at school. If the school counselor is going to modify the services provided, it would be respectful to discuss this with the parents and with the student.

COMPETENCE

Before engaging in consultation activities, consultants must be certain that they are practicing "only within the boundaries of their competence, based on their education, training, supervised experience, state and national professional credentials, and appropriate professional experience" (*ACA Ethical Standards,* C.2.a). School counselors can gain competence in consultation by taking university courses, attending workshops on general consultation practices and on specific topics discussed during consultation (e.g., behavioral problems, ADD, academic concerns), reading professional journals and books, and consulting with others.

VALUES

In addition to assessing competence to provide services, you must also be aware of how your own values and needs affect your ability to provide appropriate consultation services. A.1.c in the *ASCA Ethical Standards* address this issue:

> The professional school counselor respects the student's values and beliefs and does not impose the counselor's personal values.

As mentioned previously, the ASCA Code does not specifically discuss consultation, but this standard is certainly relevant to consultees as well as to counselees. The consultant's values are directly affected by his or her cultural/ethnic/racial identity as well as by other aspects of diversity. Ethical standard E.2 (*ASCA Ethical Standards*) pertains to diversity and also speaks to values through its emphasis on understanding how one's cultural/ethnic/racial identity influences her or his values and beliefs about the counseling (and consultation) process.

For example, you may believe that a student with English as a second language is having difficulty learning English and achieving up to her potential because the parents insist on speaking only their first language at home.

The parents believe this practice is necessary to keep their daughter firmly rooted in their culture and to be able to converse with her relatives, many of whom speak no English. You must be aware of the values you hold and how they may conflict with the values of others if you truly are to help the student. In this case, trying to convince the parents to change could drive them away from the school, which could make it difficult, if not impossible, for you to provide appropriate services. Also, it would not be respectful of their values. To help the student achieve success at school, you must find a way to work within the parameters of the parents' values.

FEES FOR SERVICES

If you provide consultation services outside of school hours, fees must not be charged to persons who are entitled to these services through the school. For example, providing a parent education group in the evening for a fee would be unethical if the parents were in your school's attendance area. The *ASCA Ethical Standards* (F.1.f) states that the professional school counselor "does not use his/her professional position to recruit or gain clients, consultees. . . ."

ADDITIONAL CONSIDERATIONS

Little mention has been made of specific legal requirements affecting school counselors. The reason for this is that laws vary from state to state and may be amended more frequently than ethical standards. Most school systems have an attorney who can answer specific questions for you. It is also helpful to request that the attorney conduct a workshop for school counselors on state laws that affect counseling practice in the schools.

School counselors must also be aware of school board or local school policies that pertain to them. For example, some school systems require counselors to contact parents if they become aware of student sexual activity. These policies may conflict with the counselor's ethical responsibility regarding confidentiality. Sometimes compromises can be worked out, but it is essential to follow the principles stated below regarding ethical issues. Counselors must also remember that they are employed by the school board and not following board policy can result in dismissal.

Codes of ethics are constantly evolving and changing. It is up to you to stay abreast of current standards. Regardless of the specific standards, there are steps you can take to protect yourself from ethical problems. Remember the following three principles:

1. Do no harm.
2. Consult with colleagues and supervisors.
3. Document your actions.

Ethical standards are based on the principle of doing no harm. In other words, all of your actions should be directed toward helping others and away from harming them. Consulting with your supervisor and with colleagues helps ensure that you are working within system procedures and that you are following standard practice. In any situation in which you are uncertain about the application of ethical guidelines or in which you think your actions might be questioned, document your actions, including your consultations with others. Documentation should be factual and contain enough information so that no other materials are needed. When documenting incidents, the common caveat provided to counselors is to be certain that you would not be embarrassed if the information were published in the local newspaper. Although no one wants their documentation published for all to see, if it is based on fact rather than opinion, you are more likely to feel that you have represented yourself in a professional manner.

No amount of vigilance can guarantee that you never will be challenged regarding an ethical issue. Following the ethical standards and these three principles can, however, make a challenge less likely.

4

— ◆ —

Case Consultation with Teachers and Parents

— ◆ —

As student advocates, school counselors frequently find it essential to involve teachers and parents in developing a plan to help students. Both groups are strong allies in creating and maintaining an inviting and positive environment for the child or adolescent.

When working with students and especially with young children, it is very important to consult with the significant "big people" in their lives (i.e., parents and teachers). Your impact is greatly increased when you gather information, explore alternatives, offer suggestions, and help make plans with the parents and teachers who control so much of the physical, affective, and cognitive environment in which the child or adolescent lives. It is important to get the big people in a little person's life *pulling in the same direction.*

BASIC CONSULTATION MODEL

The five-step model for consultation (see Figure 4.1) is discussed in a "before, during, and after the consultation" format. Each part is designed to help the counselor effectively collaborate with the parent or teacher to obtain the most positive results for the student.

31

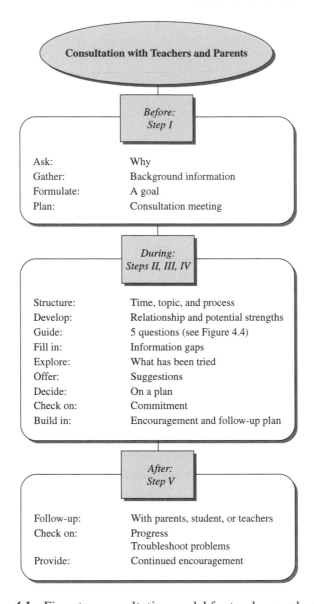

Figure 4.1   Five-step consultation model for teachers and parents.

BEFORE THE CONSULTATION

STEP I: PREPARE FOR THE CONSULTATION

Determine why the parent or teacher seeks a consultation and gather background information.

The more background information the counselor has, the better he or she can assess the problem. Listed here are several sources of background information that can help the counselor understand the nature of the problem and form intervention strategies. Each specific situation will determine which of the following background information sources are most relevant:

- Know why the teacher or parent asked for the consultation (if that is the case).
- Check the permanent record and look at:
  —Standardized test scores to determine ability level.
  —Grades for patterns of strengths and weaknesses.
  —Teacher comments and behavior ratings.
  —Attendance patterns.
- Observe the student in the classroom if time permits.
- Talk with previous teacher(s).

Formulate a Goal and Have a Plan

Have a plan for how the consultation meeting will go and some possible suggestions. The following is an example of a counselor's phone conversation with a parent prior to the first consultation. The counselor is explaining how the consultation process works.

> What I've found to be helpful is to begin by getting some background information on [child's name] from you, because you know him better than anyone. Your knowledge can help us a great deal. Next, we will spend some time getting clear on what the problem seems to be. Finally, we'll work together to develop a plan that will help [child's name] be more successful with [problem].
>
> Our meeting should take about 45 minutes. After our meeting, we can be in touch by phone or meet again to check on progress. We can decide when we meet what kind of follow-up would be most helpful.
>
> When you arrive, go into the front office and tell the secretary you are here to see me. She will buzz me and I'll come up to meet you and walk you back to my office.

This explanation of the consulting process provides the parent with a sense of safety about talking to the counselor. The counselor is seen as helpful rather than remote or intimidating. When setting up a consultation with a teacher, the same type of structure will help clarify the process and begin to set the tone for working together.

Based on the background information regarding the student and your previous conversation with the parent or teacher, the counselor begins to develop possible suggestions. Write these down on a pad of paper that you can have on your desk. During the consultation, you may decide to share suggestions as originally conceived or to modify them based on information obtained during the consultation.

DURING THE CONSULTATION

STEP II: DEFINE THE PROCESS AND DEVELOP THE RELATIONSHIP

This step enables you to begin to structure the time, topic, and process. The counselor helps the consultee feel safe by clarifying the unknown (i.e., how this consultation process will work). The counselor helps the consultee feel hopeful by outlining a plan for the meeting that seems reasonable. The counselor communicates respect for the consultee by asking for his or her approval for how the meeting will go.

You might say:

> "We'll have approximately 40 minutes for our meeting. As I understand it, the problem is [state the problem]. What I thought would be helpful is that together we get clear on what the problem involves and what is causing it or keeping it going. Then we will be able to put our heads together and develop an action plan to help you achieve your goals. Does that sound okay?"

This example shows the use of structuring that focuses on the amount of time, the topic, and the process for the consultation meeting. It reflects a relationship based on working together.

Start with the Positives

Starting with positives and strengths has multiple purposes. When you begin a consultation positively, you change the focus from critical to hopeful. You communicate to the teacher or parent that you see the student as more than merely the presenting problem.

Focusing on positives first provides encouragement as the consultee thinks, "Well, I must have done something right." Beginning with positives helps you to clarify student strengths, which you can use later when developing an action plan. Frequently problems stem from discouragement; therefore most action plans include encouragement. The "fix-up" frequently builds on strengths in order to reduce weaknesses. Ask for positives related to schoolwork, school behavior, peer relations, responsibility, helpfulness, relationships with adults, and areas of interest such as hobbies and activities.

Starting with positives sometimes does not appear logical to the consultee who is usually focused on the problem and student deficits. It is useful to provide a rationale for beginning with student strengths. For example:

> Before we begin clarifying the problem and working on an action plan, I have found it very helpful to focus on some of the strengths and positive qualities of the student. These strengths often help us later to build an action plan that really works. So, tell me about some of [student's name's] strengths.

STEP III: GATHER AND PRESENT INFORMATION ABOUT THE STUDENT

Use a logical questioning sequence to help clarify behaviors and fill in missing information about the child.

The following five-question sequence has many purposes. The first question to be explored is *how the consultee sees the problem*. Helping the parent or teacher to clarify the problem and frame it in concrete and realistic terms is crucial to the rest of the consultation. Counselors should not assume that consultees have a clear and realistic idea of the nature and cause of the problem. Usually they are aware only of some of the most noticeable symptoms or consequences of the problem.

Clarify the Problem in Concrete Terms

One way to start might be by asking:

1. *Can you briefly describe the problem in terms of what the student is doing that is of most concern?* Some helpful follow-up questions to get a clear picture of the problem are:
   —What happens just before the problem behavior?
   —Then what happens [problem behavior]?
   —When he or she does that, what are you feeling?
   —Then what do you do?
   —What is the child's reaction to what you do?
   Next, the counselor should clarify *the duration and frequency* of the behavior.

—How long has the behavior been a problem?

—How frequently does this behavior occur?

Clarify the Goal in Concrete Terms

2. *What changes would you expect to see if things began to get better?* This question helps to specify what behavioral changes will be apparent when things change for the better. This question also helps focus on small, beginning changes. This is important, because the ability to notice and encourage/reinforce small, beginning changes is extremely important in fostering positive behavior.

   This information helps the counselor determine a realistic guess as to how long the plan to change the behavior may take. Helping the parent or teacher develop a realistic time frame for change can prevent frustration and premature abandonment of the plan.

Clarify What Has Been Tried and What the Consultee Thinks May Work

The next series of questions should be repeated until the counselor is satisfied that nothing else has been tried or conceived of as a possibility by the consultee.

3. *What have you tried and what was the child's reaction?*
4. *What else have you tried?*
5. *What do you think might work?*

   This sequence gives the counselor much helpful information about *how the consultee operates with the student.* The counselor is looking for opportunities to reinforce qualities and behaviors of the parent or teacher and identify areas needing change. The more the counselor can use consultees' ideas to develop an action plan, the more encouraged they will be, and the more likely they will be to follow the plan.

Fill in Information Gaps

Before offering suggestions, the counselor can ask additional questions to fill in gaps in background information if needed. Here is a typical lead-in for asking additional questions:

"It has been very helpful hearing about what you have tried and think might work. I can tell that this is not an easy problem and that you have put a lot of energy into getting it turned around. I really like several things you have tried and hope we can build them into our action plan.

"I have some tentative ideas about helping [student's name]. But before I share them, I'd like a little more information that may help us to be sure we are not missing something important. The more I know about how the world looks from [student's name]'s point of view, the more likely I am to find ways to help."

The teacher or parent may be able to provide further information that could help clarify the problem and give you ideas for positive change. You might ask, for example, how the student gets along with others, where he or she sits in class, what time of day brings on the unwanted behavior, who his or her friends are, and so on.

The parent may be asked about the following:

- Siblings (names and ages) and how they do academically, socially, athletically; whether they are responsible and helpful.
- How the student does academically, socially, athletically; whether he or she is responsible and helpful. (Check opportunity for play/socializing with peers in neighborhood or community.)
- How student gets along with siblings, mother, father, other significant adults at home, teachers.
- How a typical day goes: getting up, dressing, breakfast, afternoon after school, dinner, homework, bedtime.

STEP IV: CHOOSE BEHAVIORS TO WORK ON— IDENTIFY/PLAN INTERVENTION AND FOLLOW-UP STRATEGIES

Suggestions should be offered only after the problem has been clarified and behaviors are targeted for intervention, and after the consultant has elicited ideas from the teacher or parent about what might work to bring about change. The consultant should be prepared to offer suggestions if the teacher or parent is having difficulty coming up with ideas that you can predict will lead to success. As suggestions are offered, keep the teacher or parent in the role of expert:

I've got an idea—what would happen if . . . ?

I'm not sure if this would work for you, but it has been effective for many other parents/teachers in these situations. What do you think would happen if . . . ?

Plan to focus on one or two issues at a time. By addressing only one or two issues, you avoid overwhelming the consultee and increase your chance for developing a plan that is clear and possible.

Offer several suggestions (see Figure 4.2) and ask the consultee which ones sound the most helpful. Do not argue if there is resistance; simply re-state the original goal of consultation and acknowledge that, at this time, it seems as if that particular idea is not one they wish to try. You may explore the reason behind resistance and try to reframe it, but do not keep pushing if resistance is strong.

Be sure to *build in encouragement.* An encouraged person is a person with the energy and hope to try new things. A feeling of encouragement is critical to the consultee's ability to take positive action. Reinforce any positive qualities that you have noticed during the meeting. Give several concrete ways to be encouraging to the student. One technique for improving the chances that the parent or teacher will stick with the plan is to suggest that they not expect the plan to go perfectly or to work the first time it is tried. Build in the expectation that this may take several attempts before change occurs. Also emphasize the need to be looking for even the smallest improvements and communicate those improvements to the student.

Clarify a Plan for Intervention and Follow-Up

Clarify who will do what and when. It is not unusual for the counselor to become part of the intervention, such as meeting individually with the student or inviting the student to participate in group counseling. The counselor may also take on the responsibility for arranging for a mentor, tutor, or other service. When this occurs, the process changes from consultation to a collaborative effort. Set a time to get back in touch, either in person or by phone, to check on progress. This first follow-up is very important and usually occurs 7 to 10 days after the consultation meeting. Ask the consultee to contact you at a certain time and day convenient for him and you. Write this time on your calendar in his presence. Ask if he needs something to write on if he does not automatically record the follow-up time and date.

Student: _____ Date: _____

Teacher: _____

____ Confer with student.

____ Hold parent conference/ phone call.

____ Use assignment book.

____ Use contract (daily/ weekly).

____ Refer to counselor.

____ Refer to group.

____ Provide peer tutoring.

____ Schedule teacher tutoring after school.

____ Keep anecdotal record.

____ Maintain Friday contact with parent.

____ Change seating:

    ____ Close to teacher.

    ____ Quiet corner.

____ Call for time out.

____ Avoid power struggles.

____ Use encouragement.

____ Ignore inappropriate behavior.

____ Give alternative assignments.

____ Adjust material to student's level.

____ Use oral versus written tests/ assignments when possible.

____ Give assignments that appeal to different learning styles: visual, auditory, kinesthetic.

____ Provide opportunity for group work and/or study buddy.

____ Allow additional time to complete assignments.

____ Monitor first part of assignment to be sure it is understood.

____ Provide opportunities for individual recognition in other tasks: bulletin boards, errands, taking attendance, put in a helping role with younger student.

____ Help student with study skills (see "Student Success Skills: Seven Keys to Mastering Any Course," Figure 9.1 on page 99).

Figure 4.2 Plan for improvement.

Consultation Record Form

Parent or teacher: _____

Student: _____ Grade: _____

Problem/concern:

Background information:

- Strengths

- Standardized test score results, grades, attendance

- Other

Summary of consultation:

- What has been tried:

- Action plan:

- Follow-up: (who, what, when)

Figure 4.3   Consultation record form.

Many counselors find it useful to record key points of a consultation and give a copy of that record to the parent. If you take notes on the *Consultation Record Form* (see Figure 4.3) or some other form, explain its purpose and let the parent know he or she will get a copy.

AFTER THE CONSULTATION

STEP V: FOLLOW-UP

Follow through on any of the interventions involving you. If the consultee does not contact you on the agreed-upon day, contact him the following day. If the plan involves school, teacher, or you, be sure to have updated information to share on observed changes. If there is a follow-up conference, be prepared to troubleshoot problems reported in implementing the plan. Encourage/reinforce the parent or teacher for any effort and gain commitment to continue plan (perhaps with modifications). Set a time and date for a second follow-up if needed.

This five-step approach is a brief problem-solving process that gives school counselors a framework within which to provide effective consultation. Following all of the steps will help to ensure that the consultation session is efficient and effective (see Figure 4.4).

Guide to Problem Clarification

Use the following questions to help parents/teachers gain a clear and realistic idea of the nature and cause of the problem.

1. Can you briefly describe the problem in terms of what the student is doing that is of most concern?
2. What changes would you expect to see if things began to get better?
3. What have you tried and what was the child's reaction?
4. What else have you tried?
5. What do you think might work?

Figure 4.4   Guide: Five questions to help clarify the problem.

5

— ♦ —

Typical Issues in School Consultation

— ♦ —

Creating an encouraging atmosphere for consultees helps create an inviting and positive climate for students. Helping teachers and parents to effectively engage in the consultative process by teaching them how to refer students and what to say to students about seeing the counselor sets the tone for the interventions that will follow. Counselors should also think about how they might respond to questions that are frequently posed regarding their consultative role as well as how they will handle the resistant parent or teacher. Doing so allows the consultant to remain positive and focused throughout the process even if these issues arise.

HOW TO REFER STUDENTS

Sometimes, teachers want counselor intervention without having to spend time in consultation. They may drop a note in your mailbox or in passing ask you to meet with a student. Neither method of referral gives you much helpful information.

Because time is a scarce resource for most teachers and counselors, the first meeting must be as efficient and effective as possible. The following section involves a modified, brief teacher-counselor collaboration/ consultation. To improve your chances for success, you should adhere to the following guidelines regarding teacher referrals:

- *Teach your faculty the referral process.* Remind them at the start of each school year that when they make a referral you want to be successful in helping the child referred. Your chance of being helpful goes up substantially if you get a few minutes to talk with the person who has the most helpful information about the student—the teacher. Even if you use a referral checklist, face-to-face dialogue with the referring teacher is critically important to your understanding of the problem. Defining the problem is the first and most important part of finding a solution.

- *Encourage teacher involvement.* Even with reminders about the referring process, you may get a hurried response:

    —"I don't have time to discuss it, but please see John about classroom behavior."

  You may want to consider responding to this by saying:

    —"Sure, I'll be glad to see John. I know you're tied up now, could you stop by right after the students leave or first thing in the morning, so you can fill me in before I meet with John?"

  Most of the time, this is sufficient. However, if you meet with resistance you might respond:

    —"I know you want me to be helpful, but I can't be as helpful as you or I want me to be without your input."

  Before meeting with the teacher, review and follow the *Case Consultation Guidelines* in Chapter 4. Leave the meeting by thanking the teacher for his or her time and, if you will be seeing the student, *instructions about what to tell the student* about your involvement (see what parents and teachers can tell students about seeing the counselor).

- *Let teachers know what to expect with regard to follow-up.* Follow-up could involve the counselor working with John individually or in a small group; further teacher consultation where teacher interventions could be explored more fully; parent consultation; team consultation; referral for additional services; or any combination of these techniques.

In summary, teach your faculty how the referral process works, including the importance of talking with them about the student. Don't make a practice of seeing students referred by teachers without talking to the teacher first. When talking to teachers, get very specific about how they view the problem, especially the goal of the consultation. For example, you might say, "What would be different if things began to get better?" Ask the teacher to clarify to the student why he or she is being referred to the counselor. Set up positive expectations about meeting with the counselor. Finally, give feedback to the teacher about your meeting with the student, and involve the teacher in future plans.

WHAT PARENTS AND TEACHERS CAN TELL STUDENTS ABOUT SEEING THE COUNSELOR

When a school counselor is consulting with parents or teachers, they might request that the counselor meet with the student. What the student is told about seeing the counselor can begin to create a sense of trust and control that will carry over into the counseling process. Some key points to keep in mind:

- Help the parent/teacher set positive expectations about seeing you, especially that you are friendly, easy to talk to, and helpful.
- Have them communicate to students that you know a lot about these kinds of issues and have helped other students in similar situations.
- Build in control for the student: "You don't have to share anything you don't want. Just go and meet the counselor and hear what he or she has to say."
- Clarify how coming to see a counselor occurs (i.e., hall pass, you come by their room).
- *Don't* comply with the request not to tell the student that the parent called or that the teacher has come to see you and asked you to see the student.

When this condition is added to the request for you to see the student, problems surrounding trust can develop from the onset of the counseling relationship.

One way to encourage parents to communicate positively and openly about meeting with the counselor is to provide something specific for them to say to the student:

> I understand that you are concerned that Judy might be upset with you for talking to me about this. However, it has been my experience that not being up front with students about why I asked to see them usually backfires. They usually figure out at some point that both you (parents) and I were not being totally honest. Then the trust I need to work with them is gone and they still

are mad at you (parents). The process works much better when parents tell their children why they are concerned. Tell Judy you know that I talk to lots of students about these kinds of things and you would like her to come and see me.

Expect your daughter to resist the idea of coming to talk with someone she doesn't know very well. This is normal and healthy. To help give her some sense of control, tell her she can decide how much, if anything, to say to me, but that you just want her to come to see me and hear what I have to say. Let her know that her teacher said I was very friendly and easy to talk to, and that lots of students feel better after seeing me.

Let her know that I will see her tomorrow morning at nine o'clock. Her teacher will give her a pass to come see me. Only Judy and her teacher will know where she is going. It will be up to Judy to decide if anyone else knows. (For primary-age students, the counselor should come to their classroom for them.)

When a teacher has asked that you see a student, you will also want them to let the student know you will be seeing them. Provide the teacher with the following instructions:

I'll be seeing John tomorrow morning and I'll let you know how that goes. Please tell John you asked me to meet with him and why. Stress your concern that things are not going well for him and you think talking with me can help. Mention that I'm very friendly, easy to talk to, and have helped lots of students with similar problems. The message should be positive and helpful and should be delivered privately.

If the teacher does not have an opportunity to let the student know you will be seeing him or her, the counselor will want to let the student know how he or she was referred:

Your teacher has asked me to talk with you about some changes he has noticed in your grades. He is concerned and thought it might be helpful for me to spend some time with you. This is something I have talked about with other students and I have been able to be helpful in most cases. You can choose what you would like to share as we talk and decide if you think this would be helpful.

If you will see the student again, be sure to clarify how coming to see you would work.

FREQUENTLY ASKED QUESTIONS

In the consultant role, counselors should know where they stand and what they believe with regard to models, theories, and their philosophical thoughts regarding counseling. Questions will frequently surface that require consultants to respond based on the personal approach they have developed. The following are some of the questions or statements that are typically asked of school counselors. Write down your responses to these and other questions frequently asked. This will help you avoid being caught off guard and allows for a response that reflects theory as well as the purpose and value of counseling.

From Teachers

- My class won't listen to a thing I say. Would you come in and talk to them?
- Would you come into my class to talk about suicide?
- These kids are so cruel to each other. Would you talk to them?
- This mother kept me on the phone for two hours last night. Parents do this every night.
- I know he has a low IQ, but I only give him half the number of math problems that everyone else gets.

From Parents

- What does a school counselor do?
- I don't want my child to miss class to go to a group.
- Could you please see my child every day at two o'clock and call me once a week.
- Do you teach values?
- I don't believe in counseling.
- How can I get my child to do chores?
- My child has given up. What can I do?
- I think my child is on drugs. Would you find out and tell me?

From Administrators

- I need you to be on lunch duty from eleven until one o'clock each day.
- I want you to be the test coordinator.

- By the way, could you do some of that icebreaker stuff for the faculty meeting today?
- I want you to identify all of the at-risk students in our school and put them into counseling groups.
- I need you to tell me what students talk about when they are with you.

Your responses to these kinds of questions and statements will depend on your theoretical and philosophical base and what you decide is right for you. Suggestions of helpful materials are listed in the References and in the Annotated Bibliography.

CONSULTEE RESISTANCE

It is not uncommon for a consultee to be resistant to the consultation process. The consultant must ascertain whether the resistance is to the consultant's style or to the issues being discussed. If resistance is present, it can be used as a means for compromise and relationship building. Do not view the resistance as a negative, but rather as a piece of information that can be used to better understand the problem. There is usually a reason for the consultee's resistance. Again, avoid a power struggle. You cannot make the consultee move faster or see things the way you do. However, you can encourage, inspire, and model. After identifying common themes of resistance, the consultant can develop strategies for diffusing emotions and helping the consultee gain new perspectives. Some themes are:

- It is the school's fault.
- It is the parents' fault.
- The child is bad or lazy.
- It is another child's fault.
- The child was just born that way.
- He is just like his father.
- Religiosity.
- Divorce or blended family issues are the cause.
- The child just needs a good spanking.

For additional information on resistance and school consultation see *The Sources and Management of Resistance to Consultation,* an article by Dougherty, Dougherty, and Purcell (1991).

Many issues, such as resistance, arise for the school counselor in the consultative role. These don't need to be seen as negative but as a way to gather additional information about what might be going on with the consultee and student. Helping parents and teachers learn how to refer and what to say to students regarding the counselor can also help by encouraging a positive process. Solidifying professional beliefs and a theoretical approach regarding your work as a school counselor/consultant will allow you to present yourself as a knowledgeable and proactive helping professional.

6

— ♦ —

Workshops and Education Programs

— ♦ —

Case consultation involves helping consultees identify ways to enhance relationships with children and adolescents resulting in improved behaviors. Appropriate strategies are identified and plans are made for their implementation. The chances for successful intervention by the consultee are increased in an atmosphere of mutual respect and encouragement and when parents and teachers have a better understanding of behavior as well as skills for communicating effectively. Counselors frequently use a group consultation approach to help parents and teachers learn more about creating this type of atmosphere, to provide information, and to teach skills necessary for improved interaction with children and adolescents.

WORKSHOP MODEL

Whether you use a packaged program or create your own workshops for parents and teachers, it is up to you to structure the flow of the workshop. The following format offers variety, builds ownership, and provides for personalizing the material presented and for transfer of learning:

- *Warm-up:* Begin the meeting with an activity or brief sharing of something positive tied to the theme of the session. Next, involve participants by having them think, write, and share their answers with a partner. This sharing in dyads is a safe way to get participants into the topic and into sharing their ideas. Finally, ask for two or three volunteers to share their ideas with the larger group. This provides an opportunity for you to tie personal experiences back into the theme of the session—creating a rational for participant involvement.

- *Ask before telling:* Before offering information at any stage of the meeting, ask for participant's ideas first. The more you can use parent/teacher input, the more it becomes their program.

- *Introduction of information and skills:* The tell, show, do model is used when providing information or introducing new ideas or skills. This approach keeps participants involved and leads to the application of workshop skills and information. See Appendix D for more information about the tell, show, do model.

- *Personalize and practice:* After information is presented, allow time for personalizing and practice by asking participants to think, write, share, and practice in small groups (two, three, or four). This kind of applied learning is essential for understanding to occur. Small groups then report their experience to the large group.

- *Process and summarize:* Help participants summarize the workshop by providing time at the end to reflect on these process questions:

  —How involved was I in the activities and discussions?

  —How did I feel during the activities and discussions?

  —What did I learn or relearn?

  —How can I use what I learned?

  It is important to ask each participant to share with a partner or small group what he or she learned and how to apply what was learned (goal). Allow one or two volunteers to share ideals for application with the large group. This provides you with an opportunity for encouragement, coaching, and reinforcement of key concepts.

- *Evaluate:* Have a simple written evaluation (see Figure 6.1) at the end of the workshop, series, or class. Use the results to improve your next offering and for positive public relations.

For more information on group consultation, see Matthes and Dustin (1980), White and Riordan (1990), and Kottman and Wilborn (1992).

PROGRAMS FOR TEACHERS

As a school counselor, you cannot be responsible for all the affective/social skills education of students, but you can offer teachers skills that will

Workshop Evaluation

Today's workshop was:

Check one:

☐ Very helpful ☐ Helpful ☐ Not at all helpful

Some of my ideas that were validated were: _____
_____
_____

Some new ideas that I can use are: _____
_____
_____

I liked: _____
_____
_____

To make this workshop even better, I would: _____
_____
_____

Additional comments: _____
_____
_____
_____
_____

Figure 6.1 Workshop evaluation. Modify the form as necessary.

promote a more encouraging and democratic classroom atmosphere. Most teachers have not had courses in communication skills and human relationship skills. Counselors can teach teachers the skills they need to promote a positive and caring classroom climate.

Masten and Coatsworth (1998) reviewed 25 years of research on helping students develop academic and social competence. They found that teacher interaction patterns were one of four critical variables that determined student success or failure. Therefore, helping teachers develop effective interpersonal skills could be one of the most productive uses of the counselor-teacher consultation time.

The counselor can offer teachers training in areas that are perceived as a need in the school, in a grade level or a department. A typical program to introduce key skills might be one-hour sessions after school on topics such as:

- Communication skills for the classroom teacher
- Creating supportive, caring, and encouraging classroom climates
- Understanding behavior
- Helping students develop responsibility and self-discipline

Any of these topics could be expanded to half or full-day workshops or a series of one-hour workshops. Many school counselors find that the most effective way to teach these skills and related topics is through staff-development courses. Packaged programs like *Cooperative Discipline, Tribes,* and *STET* (Systematic Training for Effective Teaching) offer excellent training that counselors can easily lead without lots of preparation time. These programs are very well organized and in the authors' experience have been well received by teachers.

COOPERATIVE DISCIPLINE

Cooperative Discipline (Albert, 1996, 2003) provides teachers a positive approach to working with students and parents to minimize discipline problems in classrooms. This approach utilizes corrective, preventive, and supportive strategies to create safe, orderly classrooms in which to teach and learn. The program is appropriate for use with elementary, middle, and high school teachers. It provides a framework for understanding student behavior and many specific intervention strategies.

TRIBES: A NEW WAY OF LEARNING AND BEING TOGETHER

Tribes (Gibbs, 2001) is a research-based program for teachers. It emphasizes community building and helping teachers help students develop skills critical to long-term success such as listening, problem solving, communication, team work and collaboration, and conflict management. The program is geared for elementary and middle school teachers. It provides practical activities to develop group cohesion and a supportive classroom environment.

SYSTEMATIC TRAINING FOR EFFECTIVE TEACHING (STET)

STET (Dinkmeyer, McKay, & Dinkmeyer, 1980) was extensively field-tested and is appropriate for use with elementary, middle, and high school teachers. The program is designed to help teachers successfully meet the challenges faced in the classroom, such as motivating and encouraging students, effectively communicating with and disciplining students, leading classroom groups, and getting parents involved. It provides a structure for understanding student behavior and offers intervention strategies that are respectful of both teacher and student. Although it was published in 1980, the concepts taught are relevant today.

If your goal is to improve teachers' level of skill and to help them understand key concepts about creating a more supportive and encouraging classroom, then a staff development approach, which typically involves 35 to 45 class hours, is the recommended delivery vehicle. One-hour workshops are helpful in raising awareness and teaching single techniques. However, a deeper level of change requires more time. The staff-development course, which provides certification renewal credit, is an excellent way for you to provide an important service to teachers. Teachers will come to recognize you as a skillful and knowledgeable resource.

Some of the most effective teacher skill-building programs involve a multiyear staff-development plan. The result is an entire school community using a model that reduces behavior problems, promotes teacher and student productivity, and creates an inviting, warm school climate.

PREPARING PARENTS FOR A DIFFERENT APPROACH

Consulting with others, whether individually or in a group requires you to use your communication skills. Your task is to encourage consultees to look at a situation in a different way, generating new possibilities for intervention. This process requires you to accept the parents' contributions and communicate this acceptance and understanding through the use of active listening and other helping skills.

In addition to using the helping skills mentioned, you can build specific activities into group consultation to help participants buy into a new approach to interacting with children and adolescents. One way to speed up this process is to start a parent education group with the following warm-up activity related to discipline:

- Ask parents to state the *qualities* they want in their child(ren). List these qualities on a chart.
- Ask parents to think about a time when they were in a supermarket or in a restaurant at dinnertime and to remember how other parents dealt with their child(ren). Ask what discipline methods they observed being used. List on a chart.
- Relate the list of methods to the list of qualities (i.e., does yelling help kids learn to be responsible, considerate)?
- Ask parents to state worries, or what they don't want for their child(ren). List on a chart.
- Ask what the differences are between the children and adolescents who possess the qualities we want and those who have the qualities we worry about.

After going through this activity, most parents are receptive to hearing about a different approach to discipline—one that involves responsibility, respect, and the use of consequences rather than an approach that focuses on disrespect and the use of rewards and punishment.

Another tool for helping parents examine their own parenting experience and prepare for a different approach is shown in Table 6.1. This Effective Parenting Checklist can help create a context from which goals and insights can be drawn regardless of the program used.

PROGRAMS FOR PARENTS

There are a number of audio- and video-based kits available that can be used when consulting with groups of parents. Programs are offered for parents of infants to teens. Some common themes found in most of these programs include improving communication skills, understanding child and adolescent development, increasing problem-solving skills, and learning to respond appropriately to problem behaviors. Some also include tips for helping children and adolescents become more successful students at school. Several parenting programs are described in this section.

Table 6.1   Effective Parenting Checklist.

	Yes	No	Areas We Need to Work On
I. Family relationships 1. The family eats together on a regular basis. The majority of the conversation is positive. 2. There are occasions each month when my child participates in a total family leisure-time activity. 3. My spouse and I never compare our children to others such as brothers, sisters, friends. 4. My spouse and I give our family a high priority in terms of time and do not allow outside interests (work, recreation, social life) to interfere			
II. Consistency 5. My child has a clear understanding of what is expected of him or her at home. 6. My child is aware of the rules and regulations established at home. 7. My spouse and I do not allow our child to play one of us against the other. 8. My spouse and I try to keep our promises to our child. 9. My spouse and I admit our mistakes to our child when we are wrong.			
III. Positive reinforcement 10. My child receives at least three positive statements each day from either my spouse or me. 11. I provide options to my child that encourage him or her to make decisions. 12. I demonstrate to my child that learning is a life-long activity. 13. My spouse and I show patience toward our child. We recognize that failures result from trying and are part of the learning process. 14. My spouse and I provide guided opportunities for our child to adjust to new situations.			
IV. Recognizing individual differences 15. We try to be aware of what interests our child has. 16. We know our child's friends and are acquainted with their parents. 17. My spouse and I respect the privacy of our child. 18. My spouse and I try to be available when our child needs us. 19. My spouse and I provide opportunities for our child to express his or her creativity.			
V. Responsibility/integrity/interpersonal relationships 20. I provide situations at home in which my child can demonstrate responsibility. 21. My spouse and I cheerfully take time to listen carefully to our children's concerns. 22. My spouse and I try to set an example rather than lecture to our child. 23. My spouse and I are not overprotective of our child.			

MEGASKILLS

MegaSkills (Rich, 1992) is a research-based curriculum that focuses on 10 values/traits taught as skills. These values/traits are presented to help parents help their children (ages 5 to 12) develop the skills frequently associated with school success. The 10 values/traits are:

1. Confidence
2. Motivation
3. Effort
4. Responsibility
5. Initiative
6. Perseverance
7. Caring
8. Teamwork
9. Common sense
10. Problem solving

ROOTS AND WINGS: RAISING RESILIENT CHILDREN

This program (Wilmes, 2000) is designed to help parents learn how to provide positive influences for their children. The six areas addressed are:

1. Risk and protective factors
2. Standards about tobacco, alcohol, and drug use
3. Teachable moments (improving communication skills)
4. Setting boundaries, building bridges
5. Feelings
6. Rituals and traditions

BUILDING SUCCESSFUL PARTNERSHIPS: A GUIDE FOR DEVELOPING PARENT AND FAMILY INVOLVEMENT PROGRAMS

This is a good resource for counselors who want to collaborate with others in the school and community to increase parent involvement. This manual is for teachers, parents, and administrators who want to improve parent involvement in their school. The manual (National PTA, 2000) is based on the work of Joyce Epstein and the research base showing the importance of high levels of parent involvement to outcomes such as high academic performance and pro-social behavior. Six standards for parent involvement are presented, each with practical strategies to help improve parent/school collaboration aimed at helping students succeed. The standards are:

1. Communicating
2. Parenting
3. Student learning
4. Volunteering
5. School decision making
6. Collaborating with the community

Additional information can be found at www.PTA.org.

SYSTEMATIC TRAINING FOR EFFECTIVE PARENTING

STEP (Dinkmeyer & McKay, 1997a) is a video-based parenting program for parents of elementary school children. It is based on the premise that traditional ways of disciplining children such as with rewards and punishment are ineffective in today's democratic society. Democratic methods of child-rearing are based on mutual respect and equality. In this program, parents are taught to recognize the purpose of children's misbehavior; they are taught specific communication techniques as well as ways to encourage children. Family meetings and parental decision making are also addressed. *Early Childhood STEP* (Dinkmeyer, McKay, & Dinkmeyer, 1997) has been developed for parents of children from newborn through age five. *STEP/TEEN* (Dinkmeyer & McKay, 1997b) is an audio-based parenting program that teaches similar concepts to parents of teenagers. Specific problems faced by many parents of teens such as dating; use of the car; part-time jobs; the use of alcohol, tobacco, and other drugs; and sexual activity are addressed by this program.

The *STEP* program consists of the following nine sessions:

1. Understanding children's behavior and misbehavior
2. Understanding how children use emotions to involve parents

3. Encouragement
4. Communication: Listening
5. Communication: Exploring alternatives and expressing your ideas and feelings to children
6. Developing responsibility
7. Decision making for parents
8. The family meeting
9. Developing confidence and using your potential

THE NEXT STEP (SYSTEMATIC TRAINING FOR EFFECTIVE PARENTING THROUGH PROBLEM SOLVING)

The Next STEP (Dinkmeyer, McKay, Dinkmeyer, Dinkmeyer, & McKay, 1997) is an audio-based parenting program designed for parents who have participated in *Early Childhood STEP, STEP,* or *STEP/TEEN.* Its purpose is to help parents explore the beliefs and attitudes that influence their style of parenting and to gain additional practice in applying previously learned skills. It is recommended that parents take one of the regular *STEP* programs before enrolling in *The Next STEP,* although an overview of the basic principles is included in the Appendix to *The Effective Parent,* the parent handbook for the program. In addition, a video (*The Next STEP* video) can be purchased that reviews the basic principles, explains the problem-solving group, and offers guidelines for holding family meetings.

The Next STEP consists of six sessions:

1. Taking a fresh look at your parenting
2. Building self-esteem
3. How lifestyle beliefs affect your parenting
4. Stress: Coping with changes and challenges
5. Making decisions as a family
6. Gentle strength and firm love

STRENGTHENING STEPFAMILIES

This audio-based educational program (Albert & Einstein, 1986) is designed for people living in stepfamilies. A stepfamily is defined as an adult couple in the household with at least one child from a previous relationship. This program deals with general stepfamily issues, such as setting realistic expectations, deciding on discipline guidelines, and helping the stepfamily members develop a feeling of togetherness.

The following five sessions make up this program:

1. Understanding the pitfalls and potential of stepfamily living
2. Strengthening the couple's relationship
3. Creating effective roles and relationships
4. The stepchild's dilemmas
5. The stepfamily's journey

ACTIVE PARENTING NOW

Active Parenting Now (Popkin, 2002) is a video-based parenting program that focuses on a democratic approach to child rearing. It is for parents of children ages five to twelve, and includes information about the purpose of children's misbehavior, methods of encouraging children, helping children become responsible for their behavior, and effective ways to communicate with children. *Active Parenting of Teens* (Popkin, 1998a) is also video-based and emphasizes similar concepts in the context of rearing teens. It focuses on the special concerns expressed by many parents of teenagers, such as keeping communication lines open and dealing with the issues of drugs and sexuality.

The following six sessions make up the content of *Active Parenting Now:*

1. The active parent
2. Winning cooperation
3. Responsibility and discipline
4. Understanding and redirecting behavior
5. Building courage, character, and self-esteem
6. The active family now

FAMILY TALK

This video-based program is designed to help families decide on ways they can find time to talk together on a regular basis and to strengthen their communication skills so that their time together is helpful. The program is flexible in length. There are 15 topics for discussion, but only the first topic, Family Decisions, is essential and should be covered first. This section provides information on communication and human behavior that is a basis for the remainder of the program. *Family Talk* (Popkin, 1998b) is appropriate both for parents who are new to parent education and for those who have already participated in a parent education program.

The following 15 topics are part of the program, and except for the first topic which must be used first, the leader can select as many or as few of the other topics as are needed for the group. In addition, the topics may be used in any order:

1. Family decisions
2. Television
3. Okay to feel sad
4. Money
5. Stress
6. What's a step mom?
7. Honesty
8. Teasing
9. Grandmother
10. Mother's time
11. Feeling alone
12. Mom and Dad's time together
13. Minorities
14. Equality
15. Choices

BOWDOIN PARENT EDUCATION PROGRAM

The Bowdoin Method of Parent Education (Bowdoin, 1993, 1996) is a research-based curriculum designed for "high-risk, low literacy" families who need "simple and basic" parenting skills. It is nationally validated by the Department of Education and available in English and Spanish. The curriculum is on a second and third grade reading level, fun and easy to use. Pre- and posttests are included for accountability.

The two-program series involves parents in their children's education through parent meetings. The program provides parents with materials they can take home to use with their children. The first program is designed for preschool-age children, but is also appropriate for kindergarten and first-grade students. The second program is appropriate for children from age five to age twelve and supports parents facing the many challenges of raising children in our society today. The curriculum may be used for classes or individual sessions.

Both cognitive and psychological development are stressed in this video-based program. There are 10 books in the first program and seven books in the second program, each of which corresponds to a video session presented at a parent meeting. Each book gives step-by-step methods to help parents help children improve self-concept and develop skills for success in school. The box contains a list of program book titles.

We end this chapter with a tool for evaluating parenting workshops and a tool for parent case consultation, the Effective Parenting Checklist. Each item on the checklist can be used as a discussion stimulus.

Program One (Children Ages 3 to 7 Years)

1. How to help your child develop prereading skills
2. How to develop your child's self-esteem
3. How to teach your child at home
4. How to help your child learn by looking and listening
5. How to teach your child word meanings
6. How to help your child develop emotionally
7. How to help your child learn
8. How to control your child with good words
9. How to help your child with reading
10. How to manage your child for good behavior

Program Two (Children Ages 5 to 12)

1. How to develop values for responsible living
2. Help your child say NO to alcohol, tobacco, and drugs
3. Harmony at home
4. Healthy minds, healthy feelings
5. Expanding your child's reading ability
6. Expanding your child's math ability
7. The single parent

The checklist is framed as a collection of ideas that have been found useful by many parents from various backgrounds. The idea is for each person to scan the list for ideas they think would be most helpful in their particular situation. Stress to parents not to get stuck on discussing why any specific idea is not workable, but instead focus only on ideas that seem useful.

When the discussion is finished, parents can be asked to review their checklist and pick several of the top ideas they think will be most helpful in supporting their efforts toward effective parenting. After each parent has selected the most helpful ideas, they are asked to share these with another parent. After the pairs share their ideas, volunteers can be asked to share the ideas they find most helpful with the entire group.

Many counselors find that this process of self-rating, reflection, selection of ideas to try and share with others to be very helpful in motivating positive changes.

7

— ♦ —

Other Opportunities for Consultation in Schools

— ♦ —

In addition to individual case consultation and workshops, there are several other opportunities for school counselors to use their consultative skills to affect the well-being of students. These require the counselor's continued use of a problem-solving framework supported by a respectful, encouraging relationship and the use of effective communication skills.

PARENT-TEACHER-COUNSELOR CONFERENCES

One of the most obvious ways to consult is through the parent-teacher-counselor conference. The counselor's input is invaluable in a parent-teacher conference. You may have talked with the student individually and have insight that the teacher does not possess. You can connect your information with that of the parent and the teacher. However, keep in mind the ethical considerations discussed in Chapter 3 regarding the sharing of information disclosed to you by students. Your contribution may be to teach parents new skills or strategies. At the same time, you are providing teachers with skills and techniques as they listen to you. The mechanics and content of the parent conferences are covered in Chapter 4, "Case Consultation with Teachers and Parents." It is helpful to ask both teacher and parent each of the questions from the summarized set of guidelines provided in Chapter 4.

Meeting with the teacher(s) prior to the conference will help you organize the flow of the meeting. The counselor can help build in success for the conference by encouraging teachers to:

- Have grades and any appropriate work samples ready.
- Prepare some positive comments regarding student strengths.
- Identify their goal for the meeting and prepare some helpful suggestions for the parent(s).

If more than one teacher is involved, suggest a "go around" to start the conference. Each teacher takes one or two minutes to share student strengths, grades, and concerns (without further discussion at this point). Then continue the conference following the "Consultation Guidelines" from Chapter 4, making notes on the consultation record form (see Figure 4.3). Each participant gets a copy of the form at the conclusion of the conference. The counselor is instrumental in structuring and guiding the conference.

STUDENT-TEACHER-COUNSELOR CONFERENCES

Why have a student-teacher conference? If there is a conflict, a lack of motivation, or a behavior problem, you are going to hear about it repeatedly from the student or from the teachers. Rather than deal with the problem in separate meetings all year, you can gather the parties together to work through the problem. Sometimes when a student and teacher have difficulties, it is helpful to have the counselor act as facilitator/mediator in a conference. The counselor must remain neutral and objective, allowing each person to state his or her position.

It is advantageous to meet with the teacher prior to having the student come in for the conference. The teacher can explain the presenting problem and vent any negative feelings. It is better for you to hear the anger or frustration then rather than during the conference. Help the teacher focus on the student's positive qualities after you listen to the problems.

Meet with students beforehand to teach them some skills in communicating with adults. Using "I" messages is an effective way for them to state how they feel without attacking the teacher. You may wish to role-play the situation with the student.

Use a simple conflict-resolution or mediation mode. When the teacher and student arrive for the conference, seat them opposite each other with you in between. A sample model to resolve conflicts between teachers and students would be:

- Explain why the three of you are meeting and that you are hopeful the outcome will be positive for both of them.
- Explain that you will be neutral and not judgmental.
- Explain the procedure: "Each of you will have an opportunity to explain how you see the situation without interruption from the other."
- Provide time to clarify anything that was said.
- Each person states what he or she would like to have happen. The counselor summarizes frequently and uses reflective listening to be sure there is understanding about the request.
- Each person relates to the other his or her understanding about the request.
- An agreement is reached.
- Set up a time in the near future, perhaps in one week, to see if the plan is working.

The student-teacher conference addresses the conflict directly. Once the mediation model has been implemented, you will frequently see a dramatic change for the better in the student. Often you also will see a dramatic change for the better in the teacher, for you have shown the teacher a helpful model that can be taught to his or her students.

TEACHER TEAM CONSULTATION

There may be several levels of teacher team consultation ranging from grade level team meetings and school-based teams, to referral teams for students who have not been successful even with ongoing intervention. School counselors play an important role at each level.

GRADE LEVEL TEAM MEETINGS

Counselors can arrange to meet with grade level teams at key points during the school year or as requested. These teacher team meetings can be used to discuss needs, issues, or concerns that surface frequently at that particular grade level. Counselors can help facilitate problem clarification, brainstorming possible solutions that would be consistent across the grade level, and action planning. In addition, this type of consultation offers opportunities for teachers to see how the needs of their students can be supported by interventions school counselors are prepared to deliver. For example, teachers at one grade level may express concern about the ability of students to work cooperatively in groups even though the county curriculum suggests cooperative group work be infused as a teaching strategy. While teacher strategies to develop these skills would be discussed, one intervention might include classroom guidance targeting cooperative group work skills. Embedded in the intervention would be the opportunity to model the encouragement and support students need from adults and peers to be successful in addition to introducing key group work skills. Additionally, consultation can be the vehicle to plan for carry over and reinforcement of key skills introduced.

Counselors can also use grade level consultation as an opportunity to help teacher teams develop their own network for ongoing support and feedback regarding grade level or individual student needs. Once introduced to a problem-solving process and encouraged to make it a part of regular grade level meetings, teachers generally come up with effective strategies for handling most of their concerns. It is likely that at least one other teacher (most likely several teachers) on the team will have dealt with the concern/issue being discussed and can begin the brainstorming solution-focused process. Setting up a framework in which teachers can network and exchange ideas empowers them to become their own problem solvers.

Consulting with a teaching team about grade level concerns and helping to establish a framework for addressing individual student needs is one of the most efficient ways for school counselors to effect change. It is a time to clarify, explore, and create new strategies that will affect the classroom and school climate and ultimately student success in the classroom.

SCHOOL-BASED TEAMS

School-based teams are exploratory and problem solving in nature. They are an opportunity for teachers to consult with other school staff who may have been involved with a particular student or who may be able to offer insight or suggestions based on an area of expertise (for example, a curriculum specialist or speech teacher). Facilitating the school-based team meeting is another consultative opportunity for the school counselor. In this role, the counselor can utilize facilitation and group problem-solving skills, interject advocacy for students, and be in a position to know what other school level or outside of school interventions are in place. If there are special needs or circumstances, the school counselor is likely to have been a point of contact. As part of the team, the counselor can decide when to offer her own services and when to link to other appropriate services in or out of the immediate school setting.

Most schools already have some type of school-based team in place. These teams have many names such as the school-based team, student services team, or the educational planning team. The following tips and procedures have been found to be helpful in developing successful school-based teams:

• *Member composition:* Membership on support teams is a critical factor. Teachers who teach the student being discussed are rotating team members. This may include one or several teachers. Standing members might include the counselor, curriculum specialist, an administrator (might be a principal, assistant principal, dean, or behavior specialist), speech or ESE representative, and school psychologist. It may be that other school staff are included but this core is important so that all perspectives are considered.

• *Meeting logistics:* Plan specific days/times for team meetings. This allows team members to protect time for involvement. It also allows teachers to plan accordingly. For example, one school may plan for the school-based team to meet each Tuesday at 7:30, 2:30, and 3:15. Another school may plan for the school-based team to meet at 7:30 on Tuesday, Wednesday, and Thursday mornings each week. In either case, team members can schedule other activities accordingly.

Requests for team meetings by teachers or other staff can be made through the guidance office. A request for a school-based team meeting might look like Figure 7.1. Note that the form is not so complicated it will deter a teacher from making a request to consult with the school-based team. However, completing the form does make it apparent that the teacher would have been expected to try some other things including contacting the parent (in most cases) prior to requesting this type of meeting.

It is advisable to provide the teacher with a brief notice for upcoming meetings, including the meeting time and date as well as directions for what to bring. This usually includes grade book, anecdotal records, work samples, and any record of previous parent contact. Other team members should be alerted to the names of students who will be discussed to allow them to bring any information they have pertaining to the student being discussed that might not be part of the permanent student record. This might include

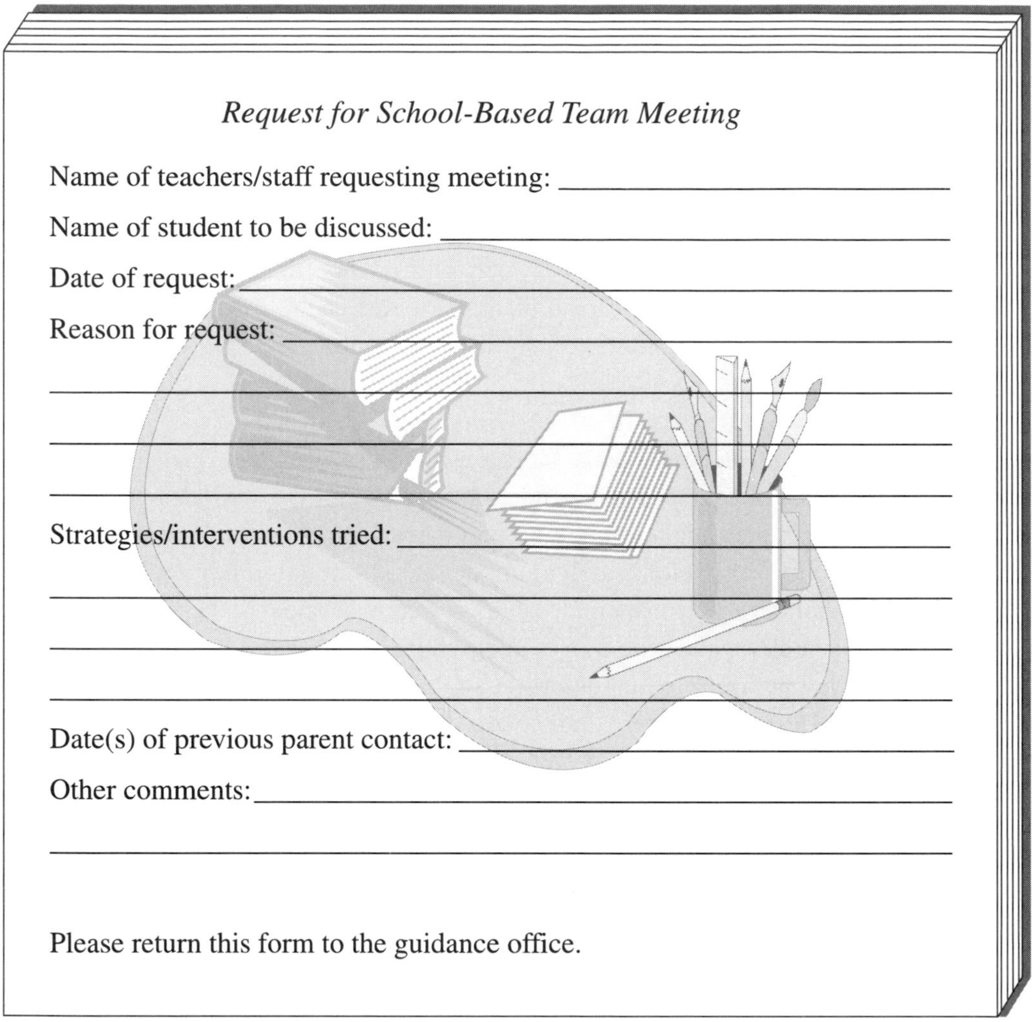

Request for School-Based Team Meeting

Name of teachers/staff requesting meeting: _____

Name of student to be discussed: _____

Date of request: _____

Reason for request: _____

_____

_____

_____

Strategies/interventions tried: _____

_____

_____

_____

Date(s) of previous parent contact: _____

Other comments: _____

_____

Please return this form to the guidance office.

Figure 7.1   Request for school-based team meeting.

recent curriculum/language screenings or behavioral records. As with other types of consultation, a permanent record review prior to the meetings to check for a wide range of information including health screening, report cards, previous test results, and so forth is advisable. The brief agenda to be distributed prior to the meeting (at least several days in advance) might look like Figure 7.2.

• *Develop or identify forms to record important information:* Many school districts have developed forms to keep track of school-based team meetings. These forms allow for the systematic collection of information regarding meeting attendance, demographic and standardized information

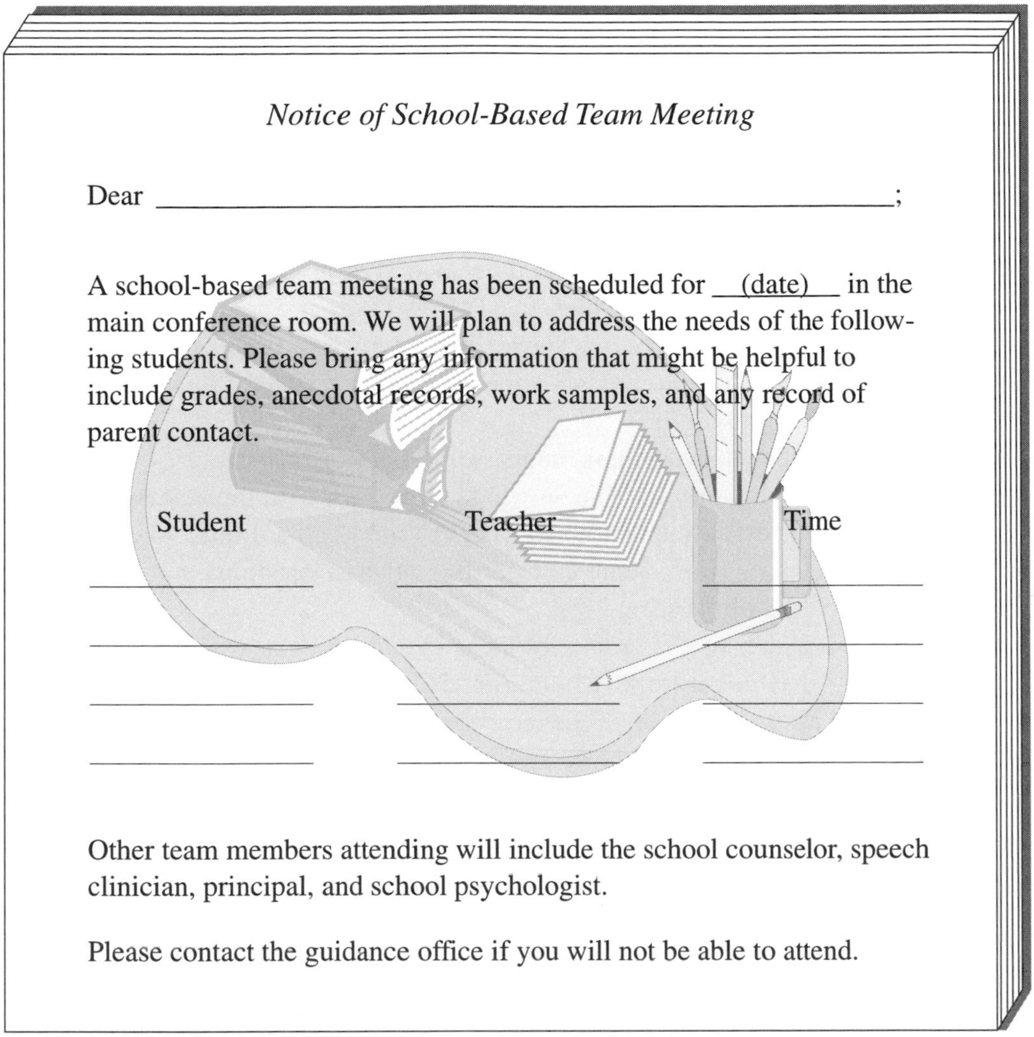

Notice of School-Based Team Meeting

Dear _____ ;

A school-based team meeting has been scheduled for __(date)__ in the main conference room. We will plan to address the needs of the following students. Please bring any information that might be helpful to include grades, anecdotal records, work samples, and any record of parent contact.

Student	Teacher	Time
_____	_____	_____
_____	_____	_____
_____	_____	_____
_____	_____	_____

Other team members attending will include the school counselor, speech clinician, principal, and school psychologist.

Please contact the guidance office if you will not be able to attend.

Figure 7.2 Notice of school-based team meeting.

about the student, the nature of the concern, documentation of plans for intervention, plans for coordination of services, as well as plans for follow-up. While the counselor may facilitate the discussion process, it will be necessary to determine who will record information and who will write up plans for intervention. One example might find the school counselor facilitating the problem-solving process, the principal reviewing and sharing highlights from the cumulative/permanent record, another team member completing the school-based team record during the meeting, and the psychologist writing up the plan for intervention and assessment of progress toward the goal.

Demographic information could be filled in prior to the meeting by the guidance aide/assistant. When the same team member completes the same task each week there is consistency and an opportunity to develop expertise with modeling and coaching as needed.

• *The consultative process:* The counselor facilitates a group discussion to include the teacher(s) and all team members. The following questions can be used to guide the process:

—What is the problem? Is it behavioral or academic?

—What has already been tried? How has that worked?

—Who else has been involved? Has there been parent contact, an individual conference with the student, counselor contact, referral to administration?

—What do you think might work? (Counselor explores other ideas teacher may have about what might work with the student.)

—Have you thought about . . . ? (Counselor facilitates brainstorming among team members regarding other suggestions that might work with this student.)

—Which of the strategies/ideas that have been explored sound like they might work? (Counselor explores this with team members who will be involved in the intervention(s).)

—Who will be involved and how can we make this work? (Counselor facilitates action planning and follow-up.)

• During this discussion, the team synthesizes goals and agrees on a new strategy. Several team members may have a role in the implementation and follow-up. It is important to keep a record of who will do what and to provide some structure and support to increase the chances for successful follow-through. It is also important to plan how progress toward goals will be assessed. You will also want to set up a time to try the new plan or implement the new strategies. For example, as a result of a school-based team meeting:

—Teachers may agree to try different strategies to make sure the student understands the directions before beginning work on an assignment. To increase the chances of a successful intervention, it would be helpful to have teachers talk specifically about what, where, when, and how they will implement the strategy. This gives other team members an opportunity to offer suggestions and give feedback about the intended plan. It may be that another team member can also offer to model a more effective approach.

—The curriculum specialist may decide to do a brief reading inventory to make sure the curriculum materials are an appropriate match for the student's current achievement levels. While the teacher and curriculum specialist are both present, it would be a good idea to find a day and time that will work to administer the inventory.

—The school counselor may have plans for a group or other intervention that might help the student gain confidence in his or her ability to be academically successful.

• *Plans for follow-up:* Steps should be taken to coordinate follow-up of plans made at the school-based team meeting. A copy of the intervention planning and assessment form should be copied and given to the teacher at the conclusion of the team meeting. If any other team members are

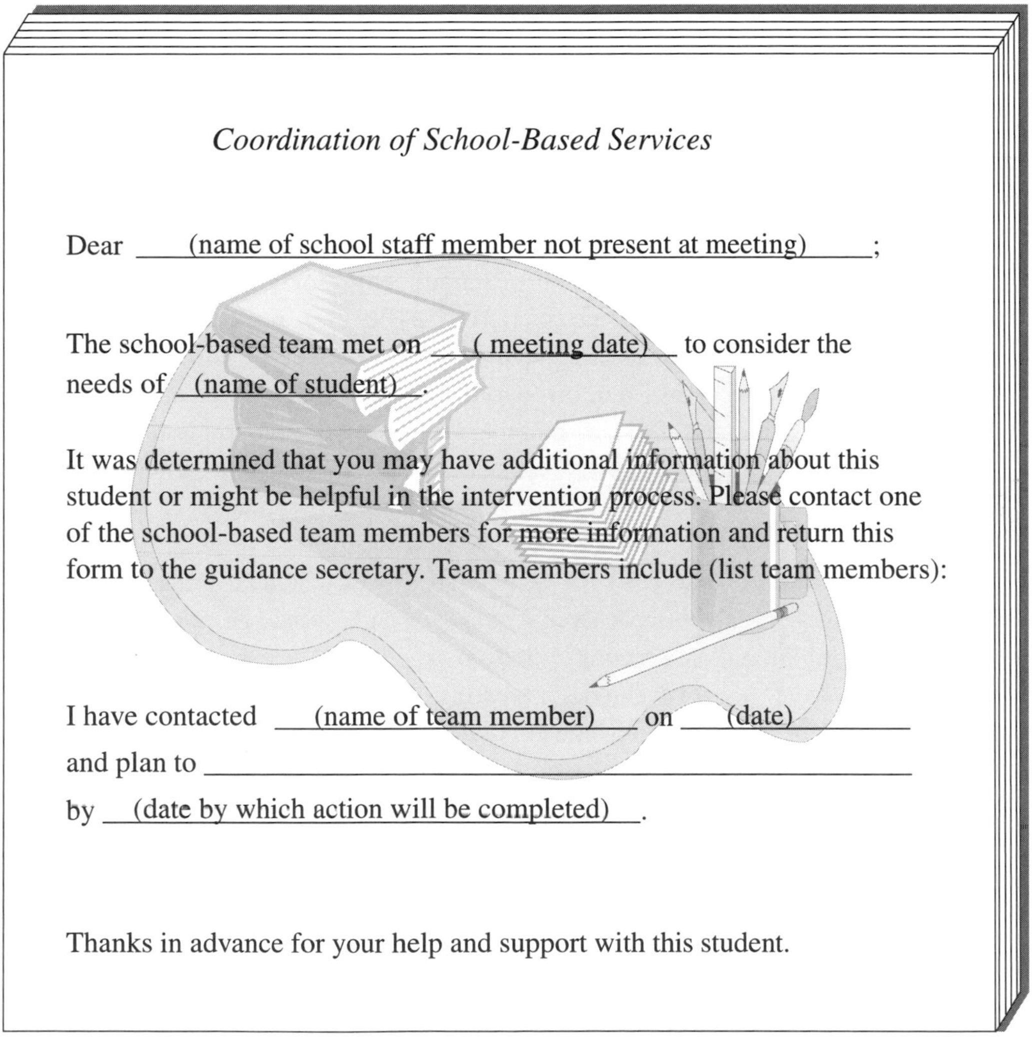

Coordination of School-Based Services

Dear _____(name of school staff member not present at meeting)_____;

The school-based team met on ____(meeting date)___ to consider the needs of __(name of student)__.

It was determined that you may have additional information about this student or might be helpful in the intervention process. Please contact one of the school-based team members for more information and return this form to the guidance secretary. Team members include (list team members):

I have contacted ____(name of team member)____ on ___(date)_____ and plan to _____ by ___(date by which action will be completed)___.

Thanks in advance for your help and support with this student.

Figure 7.3 Coordination of school-based services.

involved in the intervention they may also need a copy. Sometimes there is follow-up for school staff not in attendance. For example, the team may decide that a more current vision screening or a check on the side effects of a particular medication is needed. In that case, coordination with the school nurse may be appropriate. The form on the previous page may be one way to support coordination efforts. *All school staff should be reminded that any written information regarding students is confidential and should be treated as such.* Notes in mail boxes with student names should be folded, stapled, or placed in an envelope to ensure that the contents are only viewed by intended staff.

REFERRAL TEAMS

Referral teams differ from other school-based teams in that they are set up to specifically follow federal and state guidelines regarding the referral of students for psychological testing and potential inclusion in exceptional student education (ESE) programs. Student and parent rights are protected in this process. It is important for school counselors to be familiar with the parent and student rights associated with the referral process. These guidelines are readily available through the district office as noncompliance may involve withdrawal of federal funds to the particular district.

It is not unusual for the members of the school-based team and referral team to be similar if not the same. Although the work of the school-based team may precede referral, it should not be assumed that all students brought to the school-based team will proceed to the referral team. Only those students who have not responded to well-planned, implemented, and documented intervention over a period of time should be referred on to the referral team. At that point, decisions are made regarding the appropriateness of individual psychological testing by a school psychologist. The school counselor also may facilitate this decision-making process but at the least should be a team member whose primary concern is advocacy for the student. The following should be considered by the referral team:

- Was the intervention well planned and fully implemented? For example, we would not want a student to be referred as a result of an unsuccessful behavioral intervention implemented by the teacher if the teacher frequently had been absent that semester.
- Did the student make improvement toward the goal? It may be that the intervention did help the student to make gains and could be applied more broadly to include other contexts.

- Are there other interventions that might be tried that would likely be successful? State and federal guidelines call for a minimum intervention period (usually about six weeks) after which some teachers will want an "automatic" referral. As an advocate for the student, counselors can help make sure that interventions that should work have been tried even if this extends beyond the required intervention period.
- Is a referral for psychological testing and possible ESE placement the best thing for this student? When teacher and school-based teams have carefully explored the needs of a student, implemented well-planned and appropriate interventions, and the student continues to exhibit academic or behavioral difficulties the referral may be the best strategy to provide the additional information or support necessary for the student to have the best chances at school success.

If after careful consideration the referral team makes a decision to proceed, the formal process for evaluation begins and may include the recording of background information, appropriate screenings for vision, hearing, speech/language, documentation of intervention, observations, work samples, and parent consent. Many districts have ESE specialists who coordinate assembly of the referral. Once the referral is complete, the student can then be evaluated by the school psychologist. This can be a long process with many students not being evaluated for many months after they are referred. This makes it particularly important for counselors to be involved in schoolwide planning that creates the best and most effective learning environment for all students while working with teachers and school-based teams to plan and implement interventions for student success.

COMMON SCHOOL-BASED RECOMMENDATIONS FOR STUDENTS WITH TASK COMPLETION DIFFICULTIES

Several types of students have difficulty completing work. Some students are particularly active or have difficulty attending to tasks. Others have little confidence in their own ability and give up easily. Still others are unorganized about how to approach tasks. Some common intervention strategies found to be successful with students exhibiting task completion difficulties include the following:

- Change the student's seating in the classroom.
- Provide a quiet corner to work. (Active children sometimes prefer to be away from the rest of the class so they won't be distracted.)

- Treat the child as a nonstudent for a day. Please consult *STET: Systematic Training for Effective Teaching* (Dinkmeyer et al., 1980) before trying this, because if it is not done correctly it could produce undesired behavior. (Information on *STET* can be found in Chapter 6.)
- Teach the teacher how to be encouraging:
  —Look for small successes.
  —Comment on small behavior improvements.
  —Focus on short periods of time rather than the entire six weeks or quarter.
  —Teach the difference between praise and encouragement (*STEP; STET*).
- Allow additional time to complete task/test.
- Have student paraphrase directions for assignments in his or her words.
- Provide a study guide.
- Reduce language level of material.
- Give specific questions to guide student's reading.
- Have student verbalize math problems step-by-step to ensure he or she understands each stage.
- List steps of a problem on a study sheet or tape; allow students to refer to it as they work.
- Determine a daily/weekly goal with the student.
- Help the student keep a graph/chart of daily/weekly progress.
- Give student oral rather than written tests.
- Develop a behavioral contract with the student.
- Ignore inappropriate behaviors.
- Remove the student from the group temporarily.
- Assist the student in organizational skills.
- Assist the student with study skills.
- Provide outlet for sensory stimulation (stress ball, cloth to hold, allow to move around).

TEACHER ADVISOR PROGRAMS

Teacher advisor programs, sometimes called advisor-advisee programs, are designed to provide preventive, developmental guidance to students. Myrick

(2003) has an excellent section on Teacher Advisor Programs (TAP) in *Developmental Guidance and Counseling* (4th ed.). In his text, Myrick describes TAP as an essential part of a guidance program where teachers have regular academic assignments based on their interest and training, but also are assigned to an advisement group of about 25 students. Using advisement groups is based on the assumption that students can benefit from daily contact with adults who care about the students in a personal way. TAP groups generally meet for about 25 to 30 minutes daily and teachers are responsible for providing support to students as they work through problems associated with school and growing up. Teachers can provide a structured curriculum two days each week that reflects the school's guidance calendar. For example, an orientation unit followed by study skills, self-management, or other student success behaviors could provide the support students' need to achieve their best.

School counselors as consultants play a key role in the development and implementation of TAP. If teachers are to be part of a program such as TAP, support and directions are needed. Myrick (2003) has also outlined some keys to building support for programs:

- First, teachers need to understand the philosophy behind TAP and how it is related to developmental guidance.
- TAP must have a developmental guidance curriculum supporting the structured weekly sessions. Teachers need organized handbooks with lesson plans and activities from which to choose.
- It is most helpful when counselors can provide some preparation for guidance activities and interpersonal skills. Workshops on topics such as reflective listening or role playing can help set up teachers for success in their TAP programs.
- The time commitment needs to be adequate. A minimum of two days a week for structured activities seems to be important to keep teachers committed to the program.
- It is important that administrators understand how TAP works to support improved school performance so they can support and talk favorably about the program.
- Counselors will need to help teachers build in ways to monitor and evaluate the TAP program to make sure it contributes to improved outcomes for students.

During the TAP period, school counselors should avoid routine activities that would take away from their time for consultation, collaboration, or direct service to students. During the daily TAP period counselors might co-lead group guidance sessions with teachers, help develop guidance units based on needs of the students, or meet with small groups or individual students on days when structured activities are not being scheduled.

The steps involved in creating a TAP program might include:

- Formulating in writing how you see the program being structured.
- Selling the administration on the idea and getting a commitment from them.
- Choosing a committee of teachers or asking for volunteers from each grade level or subject area.
- Brainstorming ideas and developing a plan.
- Presenting the plan to the faculty.
- Deciding on dates and degrees of implementation. You could begin the first year with one team or grade level, gradually adding to it until the whole school is involved in TAP.
- Writing the curriculum. The same committee and the counselor could be given release time or a summer stipend to write a detailed curriculum that provides a lesson plan for each session.

School counselors consulting with teachers in the development and implementation of TAP is one way for the developmental guidance needs of all students to be addressed.

OTHER SUGGESTIONS ABOUT KINDS OF CONSULTATION

Because the atmosphere and the needs of each school are different, the counselor's perceptiveness determines what kind of consultation to offer. Some suggestions:

- Conduct get-acquainted activities at faculty meetings during the pre-planning week before school begins. You could develop activities or humorous skits that would involve the administrative or leadership team. A skit that focuses on the school's goals for the year would help the faculty become unified and cohesive.
- Provide a booklet of get-acquainted activities that teachers could use with their students during the first month of school.
- Meet with new teachers and introduce them to the counseling program.

- Have a new teacher tea or ice cream party to help new teachers get to know each other and become more comfortable with the school and its organization.

- During a faculty meeting, provide a handout of the counseling program that explains types of groups, classroom guidance, parenting seminars, and faculty in-service that you plan to implement during the year. Go over the handout with them.

- Conduct in-service sessions on topics such as interpreting test results; symptoms of child abuse; symptoms and strategies for Attention Deficit Hyperactivity Disorder (ADHD); learning styles; cooperative learning; motivating the underachiever; classroom management; and communication skills and encouragement strategies for the classroom.

Effective consultation with teachers requires the help of the administration. Begin by developing a sound, realistic plan, write it down, and then use your best communication skills to sell it to your administration. A cooperative spirit and an alignment of goals between you and your administration will promote respect from the faculty.

8

Classroom Meetings: Creating a Climate of Cooperation

Dana Edwards

School counselors usually consult with teachers about their concerns with one or two students in the classroom. Sometimes, however, teachers request consultation regarding their entire class. Discussing and planning interventions for each student individually is unrealistic. Because of demands on the school counselor's time, resources, and energy, it is imperative that counselors suggest effective techniques that teachers will agree to use that will impact the most students. Classroom meetings are such a technique.

BENEFITS OF CLASSROOM MEETINGS

The concept of classroom meetings is not a new idea. In fact, classroom meetings have been utilized for decades (Dreikurs, Grunwald, & Pepper, 1998; Glasser, 1969). Research on classroom meetings, though sparse, shows them to be effective. Sorsdahl and Sanche (1985) reported significant increases in positive classroom behavior and students' self-concepts after students had participated in classroom meetings for 20 weeks. Browning, Davis, and Resta (2000) found that students increased their number of positive strategies for solving problems and decreased their acts of physical and verbal aggression. Omizo and Cubberly (1983) found that a class of learning disabled students had significantly higher aspirations for learning and appeared more interested and satisfied with school when compared to a class of learning disabled students who did not participate in class meetings. Dougherty (1980) suggests that classroom meetings are especially appropriate for middle school youth and can be used to assist in dealing with developmental tasks such as acceptance of body changes, acceptance or rejection of culturally prescribed sex roles, and forming and maintaining healthy peer relationships. Lewis, Schaps, and Watson (1996) reported that schools supporting activities such as classroom meetings, service learning, and a problem-solving approach to discipline had students who had a strong motivation to learn and who liked school. In addition, these students were less likely to be involved in delinquent activities and drug use.

THE CLASSROOM MEETING FORMAT

There are various classroom meeting formats; however, the format suggested by Nelsen, Lott, and Glenn (1993), with a few modifications, works especially well. This modified format includes:

1. Compliments and appreciations
2. Conflict resolution, skill building activity
3. Old business
4. New business
5. Classroom encouragement or connecting activity

The compliments and appreciations section is designed for both students and the teacher to give compliments ("I like the way you . . ." or "You are good at . . .") and to express appreciation ("Thank you for . . .") to each other. Teachers can model how to give compliments and appreciation. They can also model how to respond when a compliment or appreciation is given by saying "thank you" and "you're welcome."

Teachers can consult any number of resources (Committee for Children, 2002; Kreidler, 1994; Schmidt & Friedman, 1990) for conflict resolution activities. These activities take 10 to 20 minutes and should include role playing to encourage skill acquisition.

Old business is a time to follow up on previously solved problems and new business is a time to introduce new problems. It is helpful if students sign up ahead of time on the problem-solving agenda (see Figure 8.1) rather than simply raise their hand to discuss a problem. Also, teachers can suggest problems for the class to solve, such as lining up quietly, turning in assignments on time, and taking notes during a lecture. In addition, new business is a time when the teacher can allow students to participate in classroom decisions such as when to schedule tests, places to go on a field trip, or how to arrange the room.

The encouragement or connecting activity is a time for the class to build cohesion or participate in a ritual activity such as sharing a snack, saying the class cheer, or using an icebreaker/energizer activity. (See Table 8.1 for examples of this type of activity.) For a comprehensive discussion of this format, readers can refer to Edwards and Mullis (2003). The school counselor should encourage the teacher to commit 20 to 45 minutes, depending on the age of the students, once a week to class meetings.

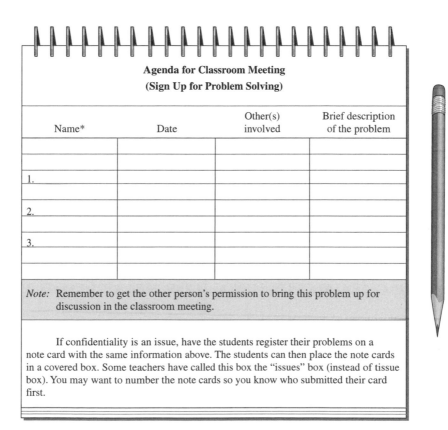

Figure 8.1   Problem-solving agenda.

Table 8.1   Classroom Encouragement/Connection Activities

Whereas the compliments/appreciations section of the classroom meeting is optional and gives encouragement only to some of the students, the encouragement activity gives encouragement to the entire class. The teacher usually designs these activities, but the class should be consulted for ideas. The following are several classroom encouragement activities.

Personal notes from the teacher/counselor. The teacher writes a short personal note to each student and distributes the notes during the classroom meeting or puts them in each student's desk before class begins. The notes might say "you've really improved your handwriting this week" or "thank you for helping me pass out papers yesterday" or "thank you for coming in each morning with a smile on your face."

You are really good at _____ guessing game. The teacher writes a statement about what each student is good at, or the students themselves can write this. Then the teacher reads each statement, and the class tries to guess whom that statement describes. For example, the teacher might say, "Who is really good at listening to others in the classroom?" or "Who is a really good basketball player?" or "Who is really good at drama?" Students enjoy this game and making mistakes (i.e., guessing the wrong name) actually makes students feel good.

Affirmation signs. The teacher writes each student's name on a piece of construction paper and hangs the papers around the room. Then the students are asked to write a compliment or encouraging statement by each student's name. Teachers may want to list examples of statements on the board and in some cases the teacher may want to proofread the statements before giving them out to the students. There are several variations of this activity. The signs can be hung on each student's back. Other students write affirming statements on the paper. This is the opposite of "kick me" signs. Another variation for younger students is to construct the signs in the shape of hearts for Valentine's Day, feathers around a turkey for Thanksgiving, or snowflakes for winter.

Charades. Each student is given the opportunity to act out, without talking, something that they do well. Others guess what it is.

Show and tell. Students bring in items of significance to "show off." This gives the students permission to brag about something of which they feel proud.

These are only examples of the possibilities. Students are good at brainstorming activities. Once teachers start creating their own classroom encouragement activities, they may want to make a booklet of all the ideas and distribute them to other teachers.

TEACHING TEACHERS TO USE CLASSROOM MEETINGS

The school counselor can teach teachers how to conduct classroom meetings by demonstrating their use while providing classroom guidance or providing staff development training to the entire faculty. One of the most effective strategies for encouraging the schoolwide use of classroom meetings is to ask for a few volunteers to undergo training, implement the meetings in their classrooms, videotape these meetings, and agree to assist in the training of the rest of the faculty.

In this process, the counselor has allies in encouraging the use of classroom meetings and actual videotapes to demonstrate their use. Additionally, this original group of volunteers can give input to the school counselor on how to best proceed with initial and follow-up teacher training and provide ongoing support to teachers. A sample survey for teachers to complete is provided (see Figure 8.2). It is suggested that the school counselor find ways for teachers to earn continuing education credit or staff development

Teacher Survey on Class Meetings

Check one: ☐ Homeroom teacher ☐ Other

Grade: _____

Please circle your answer to each statement.

Category	Strongly Agree	Agree	Disagree	Strongly Disagree
1. I hold class meetings every week.				
2. My class meetings follow the model taught in preplanning training.				
3. I have enjoyed having class meetings.				
4. My students have enjoyed the class meetings.				
5. I was eager to use class meetings at the beginning of the year.				
6. I am hesitant to use class meetings.				
7. I believe class meetings have reduced classroom disruptions.				
8. I believe class meetings have reduced school disruptions.				
9. I believe class meetings have increased a sense of belonging in students.				
10. I want to continue to use class meetings next year.				
11. I would like further training in class meetings.				

Figure 8.2   Evaluation of classroom meetings teacher survey.

units and even stipend payment if the training occurs in the summer months or after school hours.

BARRIERS TO EFFECTIVE CLASSROOM MEETINGS AND STRATEGIES TO OVERCOME THEM

Perhaps the biggest barrier to teachers implementing classroom meetings is their belief that doing so will take too much time. This is an understandable concern given the time pressures teachers experience. To overcome this, the counselor can emphasize that once classroom meetings are established, the teacher gains time. Instead of complaining to the teacher, students write their problems on the agenda. Because of the compliments/appreciations time and connecting activities, students feel a stronger sense of belonging, thus having less need to act out in uncooperative ways.

Another barrier to effective classroom meetings is the teacher's hesitation to get the students into a circle. Often, teachers do not want to take the time to rearrange the room or they do not have a room that is conducive to a circle, such as a portable classroom or trailer. Because seating the students in a circle is critical to effective class meetings, the school counselor should brainstorm solutions such as holding the class meeting in another teacher's class or the media center or help the teacher understand that with practice, students are capable of moving their desks and getting their chairs into a circle.

One concern occasionally voiced by teachers is that even though they may teach problem-solving skills, the students' parents reward aggressive behavior. In other words, some parents may tell their children to hit rather than back down from a fight. School counselors have often wrestled with this same issue. The school counselor can empathize with the teacher regarding this dilemma and offer suggestions. It is a good idea to inform parents of the classroom meeting process and try to get their understanding that certain behaviors are expected at school and that these behaviors will be taught in the classroom meeting. It takes time, practice, and encouragement to learn new pro-social skills. Classroom meetings allow students to learn and receive encouragement from one another during this process.

Another concern of teachers is their lack of confidence to facilitate the problem-solving section of class meetings. They are often worried that students will bring up problems that are "too private" or offer inappropriate suggestions. Most of us don't like surprises. To limit the surprise effect of the problems brought up, it is critical to emphasize having the students write their problems on the agenda *prior* to the meeting. This way if there is a problem the teacher does not feel comfortable discussing with the class, the teacher can suggest the student discuss it with the school counselor instead. In the case where students purposely give an inappropriate solution (such as hit back), teachers should list the solution on the board just as they do all the other solutions. When the pros and cons of each solution are discussed, this inappropriate solution will be seen as not viable. If in a subsequent meeting, this same inappropriate solution is given, the teacher can say that this solution has already been discussed and the class decided it had more cons than pros and that the class decided that this solution is not helpful; therefore, this solution will no longer be accepted.

Class meetings can be an extremely useful consultation tool. When the school counselor teaches them to the entire faculty, the school counselor can impact the total student population. A school that supports a democratic, caring atmosphere is a school where students feel a sense of belonging and thrive academically, socially, and emotionally.

9
— ♦ —

Consultation with Administrators

— ♦ —

To conduct an effective developmental guidance program in the schools, counselors must have the support of their administrators. The first step in gaining this support is defining your role and presenting your program to your administrator. This may be your first consultation session.

Using your consultation skills to establish a positive working relationship with your principal serves as the cornerstone for your consultation program. In some cases, you must use all of your helping skills to convince your administrator of the value of consultation with parents and teachers. On the other end of the continuum, and most commonly, principals view consultation as an integral component of your program. Therefore, your consultation with your principal may address plans for successful consultation and school policies related to consultation.

Defining your role as a school counselor is essential in developing a working relationship with your principal. Ascertain the goals for the school that the principal has set and then make clear that your ideas and expertise can help the principal achieve those goals. This will enhance your chances of gaining support for your program.

Sharing your ideas for training and consulting with teachers and parents is a good place to start. You can discuss how activities such as parent-education groups, teacher training in classroom management skills, and case management consultation with all school personnel will influence student achievement. If

89

your principal can see that you will have a positive impact on the learning climate, she or he will probably support you and your program.

School counselors often are members of the school leadership team. Being a contributing member of this group can help keep the counselor in a counseling, as opposed to an administrative, role. The counselor can provide ideas about how he or she can help carry out the plans being made within the boundaries of the counseling program. By demonstrating effective counseling/leadership skills, such as listening, reflecting and summarizing points made by others, resolving conflicts, and making decisions, school counselors show that these skills are useful and effective. By so doing, not only will counselors be viewed as valuable team members, but also the administration will be likely to acknowledge the benefit of teaching these skills to others through workshops and classroom guidance activities.

School counselors also should develop plans with the leadership team that map out responsibilities for effectively managing crises. Guidelines and resources for developing and responding to a crisis are provided in this chapter.

CRISIS INTERVENTION: PLANNING FOR AND RESPONDING TO A CRISIS

There are many types of crises to which school counselors need to be prepared to respond, for example: a shooting, a suicide, a bomb threat, a car or school bus accident, a terrorist attack, a natural disaster, a hazardous material spill, or a child abuse case.

THE ROLE OF THE SCHOOL COUNSELOR

According to ASCA's (2000) position statement on critical incident response, "The professional school counselor's central role is to respond to and advocate for the emotional needs of all persons affected by the crisis."

"My experience suggests that the majority of the certified and classified staff will look to the professional school counselor for leadership and direction immediately following any tragedy affecting the school community. This is an awesome responsibility but one that's much easier to cope with when you realize you have a team ready and willing to help" (Smith, 2003, pp. 14–15).

Watts and Thomas's (1998) seven-part plan to guide counselors and their school's crisis management team in developing a response plan is shown in Table 9.1.

Table 9.1   Seven-Part Crisis Management Plan

1. Crisis Checklist

    A. List of team members. Suggested list includes:
    Principal
    School secretary
    School counselor, school social worker, school psychologist, school nurse
    Teacher for each grade level
    PTA president

    B. List of updated school and community resources with emergency telephone numbers.
    Examples include:
    District secretary
    District crisis response leader and student services leader
    District transportation director
    Community mental health agency leader
    Local police and fire contacts

    C. List of individual protocols and steps for crisis management.

    D. List of steps for a variety of situations that could happen.

2. Documentation Log

    One person responsible for recording events of the crisis (names, description of the incident, chronological list of events, and needed changes for next time).

3. Facilities Plan

    Up-to-date floor plan with room assignments along with designated crisis counseling rooms, location for media and evacuation plan

4. Telephone Tree

    This tree should be updated at all times and in the hands of all faculty and staff.

5. Media Guidelines

    A. One person should be in charge of the media.

    B. This spokesperson should have a written statement and release only factual information.

    C. Do not disclose personal information about any faculty, staff, or student.

    D. Do not permit interviews with anyone other than this designated person.

    E. Nothing is "off the record."

6. Telephone Inquiries
    A fact sheet should be provided to all secretaries who answer the phone.

7. Sample Memos
    Memos, announcements, letters to parents should be ready to help adults know how to understand children's and teens' reactions to trauma and grief.

GUIDELINES FOR RESPONDING TO A CRISIS

The following guidelines are adapted from Poland and McCormick (1999):

- If crisis occurs at school when students are present, assist in getting all students inside their classrooms to insure they are safe and accounted for.
- Triage students into groups to receive assistance by:
  —Those injured
  —Those who witnessed the event
  —Those emotionally close to the victims
  —Those known to be at risk or to have suffered a recent loss
- Designate times and places for students to receive counseling services during the school day for as long as there is a need.
- Provide a forum for students to express their feelings about the crisis.
- Examples include writing, drawing, and small group discussions.
- Communicate with parents of affected students. Provide materials and contact numbers for additional services within the community.
- Coordinate school district personnel (school counselors from other schools, school psychologists, social workers) and community agency counseling services and insure adequate space and privacy.
- Debrief faculty often and provide opportunities for support to deal with individual issues and concerns. Designate areas and times during the school day for teachers and staff to access counseling services.
- Use the daily attendance report to identify who may be out of school because of the crisis. Offer support in helping these students transition back to school.
- Seek your own support if needed.

SCHOOLWIDE PLANS

In addition to planning for crisis intervention, school counselors can serve as an integral part of schoolwide planning (preventive and developmental) designed to enhance student performance, student self-esteem, school climate, and teacher effectiveness. The school counselor's consultative role can include facilitation of the schoolwide planning process, as well as being a contributing team member with expertise in behavior and social

Web Sites with Links to
Resources Related to Crisis Prevention and Response

www.schoolcounselor.org
 ASCA site (800) 401-2404
 ASCA has made the following materials available:
  Crisis response guide
  Terrorism response
  Coping strategies for children and teens
  Student and parent support information
  Crisis Response Links
  Symptomatic Responses and First Aid

www.nimh.nih.gov
 National institute of mental health

www.nimh.nih.gov/publicat/violence.cfm
 NIMH: Helping Children and Adolescents Cope with Violence
 and Disasters

www.nea.org/crisis/b4home.html
 National Education Association Crisis communication Guide and Tool Kit

www.ncptsd.org
 National Center for PTSD Information concerning research, diagnosis,
 treatment, and more.

http://smhp.psych.ucla.edu
 UCLA School Mental Health Project
  Go to the Center Response section and scroll to "Crisis Prevention
  and Response." Click on "Responding to a Crisis at a School" which
  contains specific guidelines for responding and follow-up.

www.nbcc.org
 National Board of Certified Counselors

www.drugstrategies.com
 Safe School, Safe Students: A Guide to Violence Prevention Strategies
 (202) 663-6110

www.spanusa.org
 Suicide prevention action network

(continued)

Web Sites *(Continued)*

Other helpful resources for crisis management:

www.hunterhouse.com
　　School Crisis Management, Kendall Johnson, PhD, Hunter House, Inc.

www.osba.org/hottopics/crismgmt/cmgmthb.html
　　Oregon School Board Association

www.pen.k12.va.us/instruction/model.html
　　Virginia Department of Education

School Crisis Management Manual. Judie Smith, Learning Publications, Holmes Beach, Florida. Order Number (800) 222-1525.

When Disaster Strikes, Alan W. McEvoy. Learning Publications, Inc. Holmes Beach, Florida. Order Number (800) 222-1525

skill building. Such plans might address topics such as a drug-free school, care teams for at risk students, learning strategies and styles, or other plans for school improvement. One of the most critical schoolwide plans may involve a well-defined plan for schoolwide discipline.

THE PROCESS OF SCHOOLWIDE CHANGE

The development of a schoolwide plan for discipline requires involvement and possibly changes at a variety of levels. Administrators may need to reframe the way they see "discipline" to include a more preventative approach that meets the needs of all students and not just those who misbehave. Teachers need to be motivated to change and may need additional skills as they implement new strategies. While most school districts require that schools have some type of "discipline plan" many of these plans are short lived in practice or never really get off the ground because they require faculty and staff to change what is currently being done. Schoolwide change that will be accepted and lasting requires careful planning. It also requires administration and staff involvement and "buy in." One model for effecting change is described in *The Change Book: A Blueprint for Technology Transfer* (2002) developed by the Addiction Technology Transfer Center. Technology transfer in this context is described as the application of knowledge to practical purposes passed from one person to another. Although the context of *The Change Book* is change in agency settings, the principles that guide the change process as well as specific steps, activities, and strategies to support sustained comprehensive programs are applicable and presented in an easy-to-follow format.

THE SCHOOL COUNSELOR AND DISCIPLINE PLANNING

In 1994, Wang, Haertel, and Walberg conducted a meta analysis of the factors that most influence student learning within a classroom and found the behavior of other students to be a critical factor. This is particularly alarming when 57 percent of principals nationwide report moderate to serious discipline concerns in their schools (U.S. Department of Education, 2003). Public perception mirrors principal experience. In a 1999 Gallop Poll, "lack of discipline/control" was rated as the biggest problem facing the public schools.

Over time, school counselors have struggled with the idea of being associated with *discipline*. When discipline is necessary beyond the classroom, there are certainly other school staff such as principals, assistant principals, and deans who are in a more appropriate position to enforce school policy and make decisions about consequences. However, effective discipline involves so much more than what happens when students behave inappropriately. Effective discipline also involves the steps that are taken to prevent discipline problems from occurring.

School counselors, as behavior and relationship experts in their schools (Myrick, 2003) are central figures in helping teachers and administrators understand and manage student behavior. They are also in a position to help create a caring community of support throughout the school, increasing the chances for student success. In this sense, school counselors play an integral role in schoolwide discipline. Counselors who have been trained in a direct service guidance model can offer developmental services such as classroom and small group guidance. They can also provide intervention through group and individual counseling. However, the focus here will be on the consultative role of the school counselor.

The following are some of the ways school counselors as consultants can work with administrators and teachers to affect schoolwide discipline:

* *Advocating for student involvement when assessing schoolwide need:* Most schools have some process in place to address school improvement including assessing schoolwide needs and outcomes. Even though

students and their success are the targets of these improvements they are often the last ones asked about what is working for them. When students are consulted, their input is not always included in planning for change. The school counselor can act as an advocate for students in this process helping administrators and teachers understand the value of involving students in schoolwide planning. Giving consideration to what is working/not working for students allows them to contribute to the overall process of developing a discipline plan and communicates respect and caring by administrators and staff. Genuine student involvement contributes to the climate of caring and support that reduces discipline problems and enhances student success.

- *Providing workshops/in-service for teachers:* As schoolwide needs are evaluated by administrators and staff, plans for professional development can be made. It is not uncommon for teachers to request help in managing their classrooms and the behavior of difficult students. School counselors can be involved by offering opportunities for teachers to learn more about creating *supportive and encouraging* classroom environments and how to involve students in the development of classroom guidelines. Students in this type of environment tend to exhibit fewer behavior problems. Information for conducting this type of workshop is included as part of *Student Success Skills* training manual (Brigman & Webb, 2004) developed to help students learn the academic and social skills they need to improve school performance.

- *Providing workshops/information to parents:* School counselors can work with parents to share information and provide opportunities to learn more about effective discipline at home. They can also provide direction about how to promote appropriate behavior in school. These opportunities may take the form of information in newsletters, resources through a parent library, information on parenting classes, or sharing ideas at regularly scheduled parent meetings.

- *Helping administrators and staff understand the "scope" of schoolwide discipline:* When teachers are asked about the discipline plan in their school, responses often include reactions to misbehavior such as "we have a behavior specialist, a dean, an in-school suspension program, or Saturday school." As previously mentioned, schoolwide discipline is not just about what happens when students misbehave. It is also about the steps and strategies that are employed to make sure students know what is expected and that they have the skills to be successful. School counselors can work with administrators to help all staff reframe their concept of discipline by introducing a developmental approach that considers the needs of all students.

- *Being involved in the development of a schoolwide plan for discipline:* School counselors can be involved in the development of a plan that facilitates the creation of an encouraging and supportive environment for students as they work on the skills they need to be successful as students. They can also advocate for students and provide training for staff as they work to meet the needs of all students.

One such model for schoolwide discipline (Webb, 2004), developed around four key concepts, is discussed next and can provide a framework from which schools can work to develop their own plan. The model is developmental in nature and considers the needs of all students, not just those who misbehave. This type of framework provides an opportunity to use and share effective classroom, grade level, and schoolwide strategies that may already be in place. Incorporating these identified strategies results in a plan that best reflects the needs and strengths of the individual school community.

A FOUR-KEY APPROACH TO SCHOOLWIDE DISCIPLINE

KEY 1: The Identification, Development, and Practice of Desired Social Skills

School counselors can help teachers identify the cognitive and social skills associated with success in school. Three extensive reviews of decades of research (Hattie, Biggs, & Purdie, 1996; Masten & Coatsworth, 1998; Wang et al., 1994) point to the skills crucial to student success. These skill sets include: (1) cognitive and meta cognitive skills such as goal setting, progress monitoring, and memory skills; (2) social skills such as interpersonal skills, social problem solving, listening, and team-work skills; and (3) self-management skills for managing attention, motivation, and anger. Once identified, school counselors can model (classroom guidance) and teach (workshops/in-service) ways to help students develop and practice these skills throughout the day. It is important that students know what is expected and are given an opportunity to learn the skills needed to be successful. Programs such as *Ready to Learn* (Brigman, Lane, & Lane, 1994) and *Student Success Skills* (Brigman, Campbell, & Webb, 2004; Brigman & Webb, 2004) not only teach the important skill sets but also build in encouragement, self efficacy and peer support. One of the key tools used in the

Student Success Skills Program, the Seven Keys to Mastering Any Course, can be seen in Figure 9.1 on page 99. It incorporates the three key skill areas described above and provides a structure for student goal setting and progress monitoring.

KEY 2: Encouraging and Reinforcing Desired Behaviors

Counselors can work with teachers to help create an encouraging, supportive environment in which to try out new skills and recognize student efforts. Together, counselors and teachers can brainstorm and share ideas about ways to reinforce the desired behaviors and redirect those that are not quite on target. Some examples of strategies might include helping students celebrate even small successes with encouragement, notes home, phone calls to parents, and class, grade level, or school recognition. Smiles and simple acknowledgments go a long way too. The first two keys are intended as a developmental approach to helping all students develop the social competence they need to be successful in school. This type of approach should meet the "discipline" needs of about 80 percent of the students.

KEY 3: Corrective Intervention Strategies and Consultation

The third key was developed with the 15 percent of the students in mind who may display erratic motivation and behavior and attempts to provide a predictable structure for students, parents, teachers, and administrators with regard to corrective interventions and disciplinary action. Counselors can consult with teachers about the needs of these students by helping them understand more about the goals of misbehavior and facilitating the development of clear, logical consequences through programs such as *Cooperative Discipline* (Albert, 1996). Consultation may come in the form of workshops, conferences, or individual consultation. Counselors can introduce a peer-coaching model in which teachers share concerns and ideas about what might work with particular students. It will also be necessary at this juncture to clarify how support staff (principal, deans, behavior specialists) will be involved with students who are not responding to redirection and corrective action in the classroom.

KEY 4: Support System and Additional Intervention Strategies for Students Who Are Not Experiencing Success

The fourth *key* focuses on the need to maintain a safe learning environment for all students by presenting a support system for the roughly 5 percent of

	W1	W2	W3	W4	W5	W6	W7	W8

Student Success Skills

Seven Keys to mastering any course:
Rate each of the Seven Keys on a 1–5 scale. A "1" is the lowest rating and a "5" is the highest rating.

1. I am good at picking out the most important things to study for a test.

2. I am good at boosting my memory by:
   Organizing the most important facts into an outline or concept map.
   Putting each important fact on a note card.
   Reviewing the note cards at least six times before the test.

3. I am good at handling pressure when I take a test. I use breathing, picturing a positive scene, and positive self talk to help me manage my anxiety and boost my confidence.

4. I am good at knowing when assignments are due and always turn my work in on time.

5. I have at least one dependable study buddy in each class that I can call if I have a question.

6. I get along well with others when we work together in pairs or small groups in class.

7. I am good at managing my anger. I know my anger triggers and know healthy ways to handle things when I get angry.

My top three strengths from the list above are: _____

The two things I most want to improve this week are: _____

Figure 9.1 Student success skills: Seven keys to mastering any course.

students who are having the most difficulty. The school counselor, as an advocate for all students, continues to be involved in a consultative role with involvement in school-based planning or referral teams. These specialized teams bring together parents, professionals, teachers, and administrators to examine the concerns and intense intervention needs of the student. Not too many students will need this level of social support, however, if counselors, administrators, and teachers make a daily support plan for these students they will take far less time away from the instructional time in their classrooms.

When schools invest in the development of a schoolwide plan for discipline that meets the needs of all students, instructional time is more productive, students are skilled and confident in their abilities to do their best, and there is a predictable sequence of intervention and consequence for students who need more. School counselors, as behavior and relationship experts in their schools, are integral in the development of such a plan. What goes on inside the classroom is enhanced by the consulting relationships that are cultivated outside the classroom.

10

— ◆ —

Consultation in the Community

— ◆ —

The counselor as a consultant in the community can provide an exchange of resources that benefits entire families as well as individual students in the school setting. By getting the community involved in a school project, you can garner cohesive community support for the school. Working together on a goal promotes good public relations and creates a feeling of unity. Take care, especially if you are a new counselor, not to feel overwhelmed; you cannot be in charge of everything. The first step is to get the support of your counseling partners (if you have them), the administration, the PTA, and the other schools in your community.

If you have an idea about something that needs to be changed in your community, your job is to formulate the goal and then sell it to the people you invite to participate. The more people you involve in a project, the more you accomplish and the less you feel burdened with an impossible task. If you have not yet stepped outside your school counselor role of working with individuals, groups, classes, and faculty, begin with a small project. Here are some ideas.

REFERRALS

Together with the other counselors in the schools in your community or school system, write or call the private therapists, mental-health agencies,

101

and public or private treatment centers and invite speakers to a meeting. Serve refreshments, provide name tags, and ask the speakers to spend 10 minutes explaining their services, treatment plans, or their theories of family and individual counseling. This meeting will provide you with a list to use when you need to refer families for help you cannot provide. The agencies and individuals welcome this opportunity because it is good public relations for them—and often they do not know what is available in the community either.

SPEAKER'S BUREAU

After you have met the therapists and become acquainted with the agencies, you will know who would be an effective speaker for the next PTA (PTSA, PTO) meeting. You might choose someone to speak on self-esteem, suicide prevention, stress, or wellness.

PARENT GROUP

Facilitating a parent-education group is an excellent way to promote an understanding of the school counseling program and to foster good public relations between school and community. If leading a parent group is not comfortable for you, invite a family therapist to speak on building self-esteem or effective parenting skills. You could show videos on parenting skills or drug education and prevention.

Working with a co-leader can be a helpful way to become comfortable leading a parent group. Another counselor at your school could co-lead or you could work with a counselor from a school near you. Parents from both schools can be invited to attend and the meeting place can alternate between the two schools. For counselors experienced at leading parent education groups, working with another leader can add a different perspective and energy to the group. Special education or regular education teachers who are knowledgeable about the theoretical approach you plan to use also make effective co-leaders.

When you decide to teach a parenting course yourself, remember there are several good programs to consider (see Chapter 6). The format for a parent group may vary from a one-session meeting to a six-week, two-hours-per-session course. You could also offer a parent night once a month with a different topic being presented each time.

Counselors often lament that it is difficult to interest parents in attending group meetings, and sometimes blame parents for not being interested in their children. Meyers, Dowdy, and Paterson (2000) found that parents who were uninvolved with the school were very interested in their children and were often involved at home in tutoring and in "cheerleading" or encouraging their children in their endeavors. Meyers et al., found that going into the communities was sometimes helpful in working with parents. Offering a parent group at a community center or church might be a way to attract larger numbers of parents.

PARENT-TEACHER ORGANIZATION

Most parent-teacher organizations have a family-life committee of which you can be a part. If your school does not have one, meet with the PTO executive board and start one. Sell your ideas to this committee and let them go to work. The committee can set up programs, such as parent groups and a speakers' bureau. It can ask for funding for books for a parent library. You can provide the committee with book titles on topics such as parenting, mental health, wellness, discipline, and learning disabilities. These books could be available for checking out in a parent-only corner of your library. The family-life committee can also be in charge of projects such as canned-food drives and can provide clothing, shoes, or financial help to families in need.

As mentioned in Chapter 6, the National PTA has resource materials for developing parent and family involvement programs. You can work with your local organization to begin this type of program in your school.

SERVICE OR CIVIC CLUBS

These organizations seek involvement in their school community. You might give them suggestions such as providing a college scholarship or a scholarship to summer camp, volunteering in the school, reading to students, doing clerical work, or buying books for the library.

BUSINESS PARTNERS OR PARTNERS IN EDUCATION

This concept might be more appropriately organized by your administration, but you may want to have input. A particular company could be chosen to be a partner with your school to provide financial support, volunteer tutors, career speakers, field trips, and coupons or discounts for students with good grades or outstanding citizenship. It is an excellent way to work with powerful community leaders.

COMMUNITY TASK FORCES

Committees of this type usually form because of a perceived need of the school. One community that had a high number of students involved in fatal traffic accidents formed a task force of students, parents, and law enforcement and transportation officials to look at causes and remedies. Another task might be environmental—for example, to rid the community of litter. A more counseling-related task would be to form a community-awareness program in which parents meet and agree to guidelines regarding parties, drinking, curfews, and supervision of students.

If you find that there are some groups of parents who are less involved in school activities than others, forming a task force to encourage their involvement could be helpful. For example, if your school has a large population of Latino/a students, their parents might be less involved than others because they do not speak English. A task force of Latino/a parents who speak English can be liaisons between the school and the community and relay important information. In addition, they could suggest ways in which these parents could be encouraged to come to the school to meet their child's teachers and to be involved in other activities.

GRANDPARENT PROGRAM

Grandparents, retirees, and especially retired teachers can be involved in reading to children, being a friend, tutoring, or speaking about their experiences. Enlist the help of a PTO volunteer in compiling a list of people who might be interested. Invite them to a tea, explain the program, and take them on a tour of the school. Your enthusiasm and organization will affect the success of such a program.

KEYS TO SUCCESSFUL COMMUNITY INVOLVEMENT

Any program involving the community is much more likely to be successful if you:

1. Have a clearly defined purpose that has support from all involved.
2. Provide enough training of volunteers to insure they know how to work effectively with students.
3. Have a supervision plan for coordinating who is working with whom, when, and where, and some way of evaluating results.
4. Follow-up any interaction or program with information to the participants. This keeps them involved and motivated.

Concluding Remarks

— ◆ —

Consultation is an integral part of a comprehensive school guidance and counseling program. It allows you to reach many students and is an effective and well-supported use of your time. Consultation allows you to empower the adults in the lives of students through facilitation, modeling, exploring, and skill building.

We have presented a framework for consulting with teachers, parents, and other school personnel. A theoretical foundation has been laid with a bridge to what counselors do in their schools. Techniques, strategies, sample dialog, and forms have been included to give you the tools you need to get started.

We hope this practical approach to consultation provides you the opportunity to gain new skills and increased confidence in your ability to work as a consultant in your school. As with any skill building approach, you can expect to keep on improving with continued practice and feedback as you move from novice to expert. We hope you will incorporate what you have learned into your future or existing school counseling program.

If you have comments or suggestions, we would appreciate hearing from you. Our e-mail addresses are the following: gbrigman@fau.edu; lwebb@fau.edu; fmullis@gsu.edu; and jwhite@gsu.edu.

Best of luck!

Appendix A

———— ♦ ————

Adlerian Theory

—— ♦ ——

Throughout this book, we have used concepts and activities that are consistent with Adlerian theory. Of the multitude of approaches to counseling, Adlerian theory is the one we have found to be the most useful in schools. Adlerian theory fits what we do in schools because it is future-oriented, collaborative, and realistic. It emphasizes social interest and the importance of contributing to society. The other theoretical models discussed, such as reality therapy, cognitive behavioral, and solution focused are compatible with and enrich Adlerian theory. You also will find that Adlerian theory integrates well with person-centered counseling, transactional analysis, rational-emotive therapy, and Gestalt.

Teachers trained in Adlerian theory strive for democratic classrooms where all students have a sense of belonging. They can identify mistaken goals of behavior in students so that effective and helpful interventions can be planned to redirect useless behavior toward useful behavior. They use encouragement rather than praise, and logical consequences instead of punishment.

The sections that follow contain brief explanations of the Adlerian concepts of encouragement, mistaken goals of behavior, logical consequences, and family atmosphere.

If you wish to understand more about Adlerian concepts, we suggest reading the selections listed in the Annotated Bibliography. You can become more comfortable with Adlerian theory by teaching from the packaged programs for teachers and parents such as *STEP, STEP/TEEN, STET* and *Active Parenting Now.* Some of these programs are described in Chapter 6.

The best argument for incorporating Adlerian theory into your repertoire is that it is understandable and uses common sense. When you are asking parents and teachers to try a new way of doing things at school or at home, the results will be more successful if your approach is practical.

ENCOURAGEMENT

Adlerian counselors consider encouragement to be the most significant factor in personality and behavior change (Dinkmeyer & Losoncy, 1992). Encouragement is the act of instilling courage in individuals by recognizing their efforts and potential, which stimulates their social interest or a sense of concern for others as well as themselves. Encouragement fosters cooperation, respect, and individual responsibility in relationships.

Rudolph Dreikurs (Dreikurs & Soltz, 1964) believed that encouragement is as necessary for positive development in children as water and sunshine are for plants. In other words, encouragers accept children as worthwhile regardless of deficiencies. Improvement can occur through encouragement.

As opposed to reward and punishment systems, which recognize the end result such as a grade of A or finishing first, encouragement focuses on the effort that a child expends on any activity. Encouragement fosters the courage to keep trying and also conveys to the child that the adult views him or her as competent and self-reliant.

Teachers and parents will see positive results if they begin to interact with their children in a more encouraging way. School counselors/consultants should be the most consistent encouragers in the school. They can directly teach teachers and parents what encouragement means and ways to follow through in the classroom and at home. In addition, counselors can model this practice by encouraging teachers and parents when they consult with them. Counselors can say to teachers, for example, "You've tried a lot of interventions to help this student." To parents, counselors might say "I really appreciate your willingness to come to school to talk with me about ways to help your child be more successful." Examples of encouraging statements for children follow.

- "You really worked hard on that."
- "You may not have reached your goal, but you have come a long way."
- "It is fun for me to see how much you enjoy drawing pictures."
- "Thanks for telling me how you feel."

- "I like spending time with you."
- "You have been a big help to me today in cleaning our home."
- "I can tell that you are pleased with it."
- "How do you feel about it?"
- "You know how to be a good friend."
- "It may seem hard, but once you've tried it a few times it may seem easier."

If you would like to read more about encouragement, consult *The Encouragement Book* by Dinkmeyer and Losoncy (1992).

MISTAKEN GOALS OF BEHAVIOR

According to Adlerian theory, everyone wants to feel that he or she belongs to a group and can make positive contributions to that group. Children who believe that they are an accepted part of the family or classroom group contribute to that group's effective functioning. Children who do not feel accepted often engage in useless, or negative, behavior. From this concept comes the idea that a misbehaving child is a discouraged child—discouraged about being able to fit into the group in helpful ways. Adlerians believe that behavior is purposive and, therefore, that it is important to find out what children want to accomplish through their behavior in an attempt to feel that they are an accepted member of the group.

Adlerians also believe that behavior is holistic. By the age of four or five, a child has usually drawn general conclusions about life and the "best" way to meet life's problems. These conclusions are demonstrated by the child's behavior across many situations. Rudolf Dreikurs (Dreikurs et al., 1998) posited that discouraged children, in their efforts to belong, typically exhibit four types of mistaken goals of behavior: attention, power, revenge, and the display of inadequacy. Identifying the goal being displayed by the child requires the adult to observe the behavior, recognize his or her own feelings toward the child's behavior at the time it occurs, and observe how the child responds to corrective efforts.

Children who seek undue attention usually bring forth feelings of annoyance or irritation in adults. They will stop the problem behavior for a short time when corrected.

Children whose goal is power elicit from adults feelings of anger, or being challenged or threatened. In the power struggle, children usually intensify their behavior when reprimanded.

Children who exhibit the goal of revenge attempt to hurt others as they believe others have hurt them. The adult involved often feels hurt by the behavior and might dislike the child. The child with the goal of revenge also intensifies the behavior when corrected.

Children with the goal of display of inadequacy do nothing to elicit reprimands, and may be perceived as withdrawn. Attempts to bring about changes in behavior typically end in failure and feelings of helplessness in the adult.

Once the student's goal has been identified, specific strategies to redirect the behavior into positive channels can be devised. Many of the books listed in the Annotated Bibliography contain specific suggestions for redirecting behavior. Encouragement is the strategy of choice for children whose goal may be to display inadequacy and it is a necessary component of strategies for the other mistaken goals of behavior.

LOGICAL CONSEQUENCES

Dreikurs and Grey (1968) presented a method of cooperative discipline that involved the concept of logical consequences. Six major differences between logical consequences and the widely used discipline method of punishment are listed next (Dinkmeyer & McKay, 1982; Dreikurs & Grey, 1970):

1. *Punishment emphasizes the power of persons in authority.* Logical consequences emphasize the reality of the social order which acknowledges mutual rights.

2. *Punishment is arbitrary or only slightly related to the situation.* Logical consequences are directly related to the misbehavior and, therefore, have more value in teaching appropriate behavior.

3. *Punishment is personalized and implies moral judgment.* It equates the deed and the doer. Logical consequences imply no moral judgment and separate the deed from the doer.

4. *Punishment focuses on past behavior.* Logical consequences focus on present and future behavior.

5. *Punishment threatens and treats the offender with disrespect.* Logical consequences are carried out in a friendly and respectful manner, after feelings are calmed. They imply goodwill and faith in the offender.

6. *Punishment demands obedience.* Logical consequences permit choice within limits.

Children are informed of the consequences of their choice. Therefore, logical consequences have the training effect of helping children learn about the consequences of their actions, responsibility, and self-discipline. Frequently, children are involved in deciding consequences for misbehavior.

Here are some guidelines for using logical consequences:

- Give the child a choice, and speak to him or her privately.
- Relate the consequences to the misbehavior.
- Discuss the misbehavior and the logical consequences with the child in a respectful manner.
- Make sure that the logical consequences are reasonable in terms of the development level of the child.

It is difficult to follow these guidelines when you are angry or upset. When emotions run high, cooling off is required before logical consequences can be implemented. This procedure has a positive training effect as well, because it teaches children that solving conflicts when one or both parties is extremely upset is not likely to be constructive.

One overriding principle of logical consequences is what Dreikurs referred to as the importance of being both kind and firm in our relations with children. Kindness shows respect for the child. Firmness shows respect for us and the needs of the situation. Timing is an important consideration when using logical consequences and varies according to the goal of misbehavior. Nelsen (1996) points out that logical consequences are effective at the time of conflict only if the goal is attention. If the goal is power or revenge, a cooling-off period is needed to win the child's cooperation in discussing the misbehavior. Logical consequences should not be used if the goal is display of inadequacy.

CATEGORIES OF LOGICAL CONSEQUENCES

Gilbert (1986, 1989) provided a classification system of logical consequences:

- Loss or delay of a privilege
- Loss or delay of cooperation
- Restitution

The following section presents the three types of logical consequences and examples for each.

LOSS OR DELAY OF A PRIVILEGE

Parents or teachers decide whether a privilege (i.e., to do, to use, to go, to associate) is handled appropriately. If not, the privilege is withdrawn temporarily until the parent or teacher believes the child is ready to handle that privilege. The choice for the child is either to handle the privilege in socially appropriate ways or to lose the privilege. There are four subcategories under privilege: (1) activity, (2) interaction, (3) use of objects, and (4) access to places. Some examples follow:

Loss of Privilege—Activity

Child's Behavior	Consequences
Chores not done by dinner time	Dinner delayed until chores done
Homework (or classwork) not completed by agreed time	Delay or loss of next activity
Not properly dressed	Permission denied to go outside

Loss of Privilege—Interaction

Child's Behavior	Consequences
Temper tantrum	Adult ignores tantrum or leaves area
Interfering with class discussion	Child asked to leave area
Imposing on adult interaction	Child asked to go to room

Loss of Privilege—To Use Objects

Child's Behavior	Consequences
Clumsy handling of object	Object removed
Leaving possessions around house	Possessions concealed
Abuse of property	Periodic restriction of use

Loss of Privilege—Access to Places

Child's Behavior	Consequences
Messing up activity area	Area temporarily off limits
Disruptive while in store	Not taken in store next time
Very disruptive in store	Removed immediately

LOSS OR DELAY OF COOPERATION

Child's Behavior	Consequences
Dirty clothes not put in hamper	Clothes not washed
Pet not fed	Child not fed
Late for or refuses meal offered	Makes own meal or goes without

RESTITUTION

Child's Behavior	Consequences
Child steals article from store	Article returned, or cost refunded from allowance
Object broken	Cleans up breakage and replaces broken object or reimburses owner
Damage to expensive item	Partial reimbursement (and other consequence)

FAMILY ATMOSPHERE

The interaction of parents' personalities sets the climate for the family. Because children make early decisions about self, others, and the world based on their family experiences, family atmosphere plays an important role in lifestyle, or personality formation. If consultants understand the atmosphere of a child's family, they will be better able to help the child and the child's parents. Family atmosphere information will also help the child's teacher by providing insight and understanding.

Family atmosphere includes the attitudes and values held by the family, in addition to the general climate. The attitudes and values are typically revealed when all members of the family share an attribute (Dinkmeyer, Dinkmeyer, & Sperry, 1987). However, each child can decide how he or she will react to the family atmosphere. Children can accept the attitudes and values, reject them, or follow a path between accepting and rejecting. For example, if education is valued, then all of the children in the family may be good students. If one child decides to rebel (demonstrate the mistaken goal of power, for example), then he or she may demonstrate poor academic behavior. Also, consider the case where a student has a learning disability. Having a child who struggles in school may be difficult for the family to accept.

There are several ways to describe types of family atmosphere, such as cold, tense, encouraging, accepting, hostile, or cooperative. Dewey (as cited in Nikelly, 1971) described several types of family atmosphere that can serve as a guide for consultants as they explore issues with parents and children:

- A *rejective* family atmosphere is one in which the child does not feel accepted.
- An *authoritarian* family atmosphere is marked by unquestioned obedience and strict rules.
- The *martyrdom* atmosphere is one in which suffering and helplessness is present.
- The *inconsistent* atmosphere is one in which the child never knows what is expected and feels unsure.
- The *suppressive* atmosphere creates a world where the child is not free to express feelings or ideas.
- The *overprotective* atmosphere conveys a message to the child that he or she is not capable.
- The *high standards* atmosphere creates a world where the child may feel that he or she cannot meet others' expectations.

This list is not all-inclusive, but it gives the consultant a framework from which to understand the family and the child's perceptions of the family. It is evident what a great impact family atmosphere can have on a young child. If you would like to read more about family atmosphere, consult *Techniques for Behavior Change* by Nikelly (1971).

Appendix B

———— ◆ ————

Ethical Standards for School Counselors

—— ◆ ——

Ethical Standards for School Counselors was adopted by the ASCA Delegate Assembly, March 19, 1984, revised March 27, 1992, June 25, 1998, and June 26, 2004.

PREAMBLE

The American School Counselor Association (ASCA) is a professional organization whose members are certified/licensed in school counseling with unique qualifications and skills to address the academic, personal/social and career development needs of all students. Professional school counselors are advocates, leaders, collaborators and consultants who create opportunities for equity in access and success in educational opportunities by connecting their programs to the mission of schools and subscribing to the following tenets of professional responsibility:

- Each person has the right to be respected, be treated with dignity and have access to a comprehensive school counseling program that advocates for and affirms all students from diverse populations regardless of ethnic/racial status, age, economic status, special needs, English as a second language or other language group, immigration status, sexual

117

orientation, gender, gender identity/expression, family type, religious/ spiritual identity and appearance.

- Each person has the right to receive the information and support needed to move toward self-direction and self-development and affirmation within one's group identities, with special care being given to students who have historically not received adequate educational services: students of color, low socio-economic students, students with disabilities and students with nondominant language backgrounds.
- Each person has the right to understand the full magnitude and meaning of his/her educational choices and how those choices will affect future opportunities.
- Each person has the right to privacy and thereby the right to expect the counselor-student relationship to comply with all laws, policies and ethical standards pertaining to confidentiality in the school setting.

In this document, ASCA specifies the principles of ethical behavior necessary to maintain the high standards of integrity, leadership and professionalism among its members. The Ethical Standards for School Counselors were developed to clarify the nature of ethical responsibilities held in common by school counseling professionals. The purposes of this document are to:

- Serve as a guide for the ethical practices of all professional school counselors regardless of level, area, population served or membership in this professional association;
- Provide self-appraisal and peer evaluations regarding counselor responsibilities to students, parents/guardians, colleagues and professional associates, schools, communities and the counseling profession; and
- Inform those served by the school counselor of acceptable counselor practices and expected professional behavior.

A.1 RESPONSIBILITIES TO STUDENTS

The professional school counselor:

a. Has a primary obligation to the student, who is to be treated with respect as a unique individual.
b. Is concerned with the educational, academic, career, personal and social needs and encourages the maximum development of every student.

    c. Respects the student's values and beliefs and does not impose the counselor's personal values.

    d. Is knowledgeable of laws, regulations and policies relating to students and strives to protect and inform students regarding their rights.

A.2 CONFIDENTIALITY

The professional school counselor:

    a. Informs students of the purposes, goals, techniques and rules of procedure under which they may receive counseling at or before the time when the counseling relationship is entered. Disclosure notice includes the limits of confidentiality such as the possible necessity for consulting with other professionals, privileged communication, and legal or authoritative restraints. The meaning and limits of confidentiality are defined in developmentally appropriate terms to students.

    b. Keeps information confidential unless disclosure is required to prevent clear and imminent danger to the student or others or when legal requirements demand that confidential information be revealed. Counselors will consult with appropriate professionals when in doubt as to the validity of an exception.

    c. In absence of state legislation expressly forbidding disclosure, considers the ethical responsibility to provide information to an identified third party who, by his/her relationship with the student, is at a high risk of contracting a disease that is commonly known to be communicable and fatal. Disclosure requires satisfaction of all of the following conditions:

- Student identifies partner or the partner is highly identifiable
- Counselor recommends the student notify partner and refrain from further high-risk behavior
- Student refuses
- Counselor informs the student of the intent to notify the partner
- Counselor seeks legal consultation as to the legalities of informing the partner

    d. Requests of the court that disclosure not be required when the release of confidential information may potentially harm a student or the counseling relationship.

    e. Protects the confidentiality of students' records and releases personal data in accordance with prescribed laws and school policies. Student information stored and transmitted electronically is treated with the same care as traditional student records.

f. Protects the confidentiality of information received in the counseling relationship as specified by federal and state laws, written policies and applicable ethical standards. Such information is only to be revealed to others with the informed consent of the student, consistent with the counselor's ethical obligation.

g. Recognizes his/her primary obligation for confidentiality is to the student but balances that obligation with an understanding of the legal and inherent rights of parents/guardians to be the guiding voice in their children's lives.

A.3 COUNSELING PLANS

The professional school counselor:

a. Provides students with a comprehensive school counseling program that includes a strong emphasis on working jointly with all students to develop academic and career goals.

b. Advocates for counseling plans supporting students right to choose from the wide array of options when they leave secondary education. Such plans will be regularly reviewed to update students regarding critical information they need to make informed decisions.

A.4 DUAL RELATIONSHIPS

The professional school counselor:

a. Avoids dual relationships that might impair his/her objectivity and increase the risk of harm to the student (e.g., counseling one's family members, close friends or associates). If a dual relationship is unavoidable, the counselor is responsible for taking action to eliminate or reduce the potential for harm. Such safeguards might include informed consent, consultation, supervision and documentation.

b. Avoids dual relationships with school personnel that might infringe on the integrity of the counselor/student relationship.

A.5 APPROPRIATE REFERRALS

The professional school counselor:

a. Makes referrals when necessary or appropriate to outside resources. Appropriate referrals may necessitate informing both parents/ guardians and students of applicable resources and making proper plans for transitions with minimal interruption of services. Students retain the right to discontinue the counseling relationship at any time.

A.6 GROUP WORK

The professional school counselor:

a. Screens prospective group members and maintains an awareness of participants' needs and goals in relation to the goals of the group. The counselor takes reasonable precautions to protect members from physical and psychological harm resulting from interaction within the group.
b. Notifies parents/guardians and staff of group participation if the counselor deems it appropriate and if consistent with school board policy or practice.
c. Establishes clear expectations in the group setting and clearly states that confidentiality in group counseling cannot be guaranteed. Given the developmental and chronological ages of minors in schools, the counselor recognizes the tenuous nature of confidentiality for minors renders some topics inappropriate for group work in a school setting.
d. Follows up with group members and documents proceedings as appropriate.

A.7 DANGER TO SELF OR OTHERS

The professional school counselor:

a. Informs parents/guardians or appropriate authorities when the student's condition indicates a clear and imminent danger to the student or others. This is to be done after careful deliberation and, where possible, after consultation with other counseling professionals.

b. Will attempt to minimize threat to a student and may choose to (1) inform the student of actions to be taken, (2) involve the student in a three-way communication with parents/guardians when breaching confidentiality or (3) allow the student to have input as to how and to whom the breach will be made.

A.8 STUDENT RECORDS

The professional school counselor:

a. Maintains and secures records necessary for rendering professional services to the student as required by laws, regulations, institutional procedures and confidentiality guidelines.
b. Keeps sole-possession records separate from students' educational records in keeping with state laws.
c. Recognizes the limits of sole-possession records and understands these records are a memory aid for the creator and in absence of privilege communication may be subpoenaed and may become educational records when they (1) are shared with others in verbal or written form, (2) include information other than professional opinion or personal observations and/or (3) are made accessible to others.
d. Establishes a reasonable timeline for purging sole-possession records or case notes. Suggested guidelines include shredding sole possession records when the student transitions to the next level, transfers to another school or graduates. Careful discretion and deliberation should be applied before destroying sole-possession records that may be needed by a court of law such as notes on child abuse, suicide, sexual harassment or violence.

A.9 EVALUATION, ASSESSMENT, AND INTERPRETATION

The professional school counselor:

a. Adheres to all professional standards regarding selecting, administering and interpreting assessment measures and only utilizes assessment measures that are within the scope of practice for school counselors.

b. Seeks specialized training regarding the use of electronically based testing programs in administering, scoring and interpreting that may differ from that required in more traditional assessments.

c. Considers confidentiality issues when utilizing evaluative or assessment instruments and electronically based programs.

d. Provides interpretation of the nature, purposes, results and potential impact of assessment/evaluation measures in language the student(s) can understand.

e. Monitors the use of assessment results and interpretations, and takes reasonable steps to prevent others from misusing the information.

f. Uses caution when utilizing assessment techniques, making evaluations and interpreting the performance of populations not represented in the norm group on which an instrument is standardized.

g. Assesses the effectiveness of his/her program in having an impact on students' academic, career and personal/social development through accountability measures especially examining efforts to close achievement, opportunity and attainment gaps.

A.10 TECHNOLOGY

The professional school counselor:

a. Promotes the benefits of and clarifies the limitations of various appropriate technological applications. The counselor promotes technological applications (1) that are appropriate for the student's individual needs, (2) that the student understands how to use and (3) for which follow-up counseling assistance is provided.

b. Advocates for equal access to technology for all students, especially those historically underserved.

c. Takes appropriate and reasonable measures for maintaining confidentiality of student information and educational records stored or transmitted over electronic media including although not limited to fax, electronic mail and instant messaging.

d. While working with students on a computer or similar technology, takes reasonable and appropriate measures to protect students from objectionable and/or harmful online material.

e. Who is engaged in the delivery of services involving technologies such as the telephone, videoconferencing and the Internet takes responsible steps to protect students and others from harm.

A.11 STUDENT PEER SUPPORT PROGRAM

The professional school counselor:

Has unique responsibilities when working with student-assistance programs. The school counselor is responsible for the welfare of students participating in peer-to-peer programs under his/her direction.

B. RESPONSIBILITIES TO PARENTS/GUARDIANS

B.1 PARENT RIGHTS AND RESPONSIBILITIES

The professional school counselor:

a. Respects the rights and responsibilities of parents/guardians for their children and endeavors to establish, as appropriate, a collaborative relationship with parents/guardians to facilitate the student's maximum development.
b. Adheres to laws, local guidelines and ethical standards of practice when assisting parents/guardians experiencing family difficulties that interfere with the student's effectiveness and welfare.
c. Respects the confidentiality of parents/guardians.
d. Is sensitive to diversity among families and recognizes that all parents/guardians, custodial and noncustodial, are vested with certain rights and responsibilities for the welfare of their children by virtue of their role and according to law.

B.2 PARENTS/GUARDIANS AND CONFIDENTIALITY

The professional school counselor:

a. Informs parents/guardians of the counselor's role with emphasis on the confidential nature of the counseling relationship between the counselor and student.

b. Recognizes that working with minors in a school setting may require counselors to collaborate with students' parents/guardians.

c. Provides parents/guardians with accurate, comprehensive and relevant information in an objective and caring manner, as is appropriate and consistent with ethical responsibilities to the student.

d. Makes reasonable efforts to honor the wishes of parents/guardians concerning information regarding the student, and in cases of divorce or separation exercises a good-faith effort to keep both parents informed with regard to critical information with the exception of a court order.

C. RESPONSIBILITIES TO COLLEAGUES AND PROFESSIONAL ASSOCIATES

C.1 PROFESSIONAL RELATIONSHIPS

The professional school counselor:

a. Establishes and maintains professional relationships with faculty, staff and administration to facilitate an optimum counseling program.

b. Treats colleagues with professional respect, courtesy and fairness. The qualifications, views and findings of colleagues are represented to accurately reflect the image of competent professionals.

c. Is aware of and utilizes related professionals, organizations and other resources to whom the student may be referred.

C.2 SHARING INFORMATION WITH OTHER PROFESSIONALS

The professional school counselor:

a. Promotes awareness and adherence to appropriate guidelines regarding confidentiality, the distinction between public and private information and staff consultation.

b. Provides professional personnel with accurate, objective, concise and meaningful data necessary to adequately evaluate, counsel and assist the student.

c. If a student is receiving services from another counselor or other mental health professional, the counselor, with student and/or parent/

guardian consent, will inform the other professional and develop clear agreements to avoid confusion and conflict for the student.

d. Is knowledgeable about release of information and parental rights in sharing information.

D. RESPONSIBILITIES TO THE SCHOOL AND COMMUNITY

D.1 RESPONSIBILITIES TO THE SCHOOL

The professional school counselor:

a. Supports and protects the educational program against any infringement not in students' best interest.

b. Informs appropriate officials in accordance with school policy of conditions that may be potentially disruptive or damaging to the school's mission, personnel and property while honoring the confidentiality between the student and counselor.

c. Is knowledgeable and supportive of the school's mission and connects his/her program to the school's mission.

d. Delineates and promotes the counselor's role and function in meeting the needs of those served. Counselors will notify appropriate officials of conditions that may limit or curtail their effectiveness in providing programs and services.

e. Accepts employment only for positions for which he/she is qualified by education, training, supervised experience, state and national professional credentials and appropriate professional experience.

f. Advocates that administrators hire only qualified and competent individuals for professional counseling positions.

g. Assists in developing: (1) curricular and environmental conditions appropriate for the school and community, (2) educational procedures and programs to meet students' developmental needs and (3) a systematic evaluation process for comprehensive, developmental, standards-based school counseling programs, services and personnel. The counselor is guided by the findings of the evaluation data in planning programs and services.

D.2 RESPONSIBILITY TO THE COMMUNITY

The professional school counselor:

a. Collaborates with agencies, organizations and individuals in the community in the best interest of students and without regard to personal reward or remuneration.
b. Extends his/her influence and opportunity to deliver a comprehensive school counseling program to all students by collaborating with community resources for student success.

E. RESPONSIBILITIES TO SELF

E.1 PROFESSIONAL COMPETENCE

The professional school counselor:

a. Functions within the boundaries of individual professional competence and accepts responsibility for the consequences of his/her actions.
b. Monitors personal well-being and effectiveness and does not participate in any activity that may lead to inadequate professional services or harm to a student.
c. Strives through personal initiative to maintain professional competence including technological literacy and to keep abreast of professional information. Professional and personal growth are ongoing throughout the counselor's career.

E.2 DIVERSITY

The professional school counselor:

a. Affirms the diversity of students, staff and families.
b. Expands and develops awareness of his/her own attitudes and beliefs affecting cultural values and biases and strives to attain cultural competence.
c. Possesses knowledge and understanding about how oppression, racism, discrimination and stereotyping affects her/him personally and professionally.

   d. Acquires educational, consultation and training experiences to improve awareness, knowledge, skills and effectiveness in working with diverse populations: ethnic/racial status, age, economic status, special needs, ESL or ELL, immigration status, sexual orientation, gender, gender identity/expression, family type, religious/spiritual identity and appearance.

F. RESPONSIBILITIES TO THE PROFESSION

F.1 PROFESSIONALISM

The professional school counselor:

   a. Accepts the policies and procedures for handling ethical violations as a result of maintaining membership in the American School Counselor Association.

   b. Conducts herself/himself in such a manner as to advance individual ethical practice and the profession.

   c. Conducts appropriate research and report findings in a manner consistent with acceptable educational and psychological research practices. The counselor advocates for the protection of the individual student's identity when using data for research or program planning.

   d. Adheres to ethical standards of the profession, other official policy statements, such as ASCA's position statements, role statement and the ASCA National Model, and relevant statutes established by federal, state and local governments, and when these are in conflict works responsibly for change.

   e. Clearly distinguishes between statements and actions made as a private individual and those made as a representative of the school counseling profession.

   f. Does not use his/her professional position to recruit or gain clients, consultees for his/her private practice or to seek and receive unjustified personal gains, unfair advantage, inappropriate relationships or unearned goods or services.

F.2 CONTRIBUTION TO THE PROFESSION

The professional school counselor:

a. Actively participates in local, state and national associations fostering the development and improvement of school counseling.
b. Contributes to the development of the profession through the sharing of skills, ideas and expertise with colleagues.
c. Provides support and mentoring to novice professionals.

G. MAINTENANCE OF STANDARDS

Ethical behavior among professional school counselors, association members and nonmembers, is expected at all times. When there exists serious doubt as to the ethical behavior of colleagues or if counselors are forced to work in situations or abide by policies that do not reflect the standards as outlined in these Ethical Standards for School Counselors, the counselor is obligated to take appropriate action to rectify the condition. The following procedure may serve as a guide:

1. The counselor should consult confidentially with a professional colleague to discuss the nature of a complaint to see if the professional colleague views the situation as an ethical violation.
2. When feasible, the counselor should directly approach the colleague whose behavior is in question to discuss the complaint and seek resolution.
3. If resolution is not forthcoming at the personal level, the counselor shall utilize the channels established within the school, school district, the state school counseling association and ASCA's Ethics Committee.
4. If the matter still remains unresolved, referral for review and appropriate action should be made to the Ethics Committees in the following sequence:
   • state school counselor association
   • American School Counselor Association
5. The ASCA Ethics Committee is responsible for:
   • Educating and consulting with the membership regarding ethical standards

- Periodically reviewing and recommending changes in code
- Receiving and processing questions to clarify the application of such standards; Questions must be submitted in writing to the ASCA Ethics chair.
- Handling complaints of alleged violations of the ethical standards. At the national level, complaints should be submitted in writing to the ASCA Ethics Committee, c/o the Executive Director, American School Counselor Association, 1101 King St., Suite 625, Alexandria, VA 22314.

Appendix C

—— ♦ ——

The American Counseling Association Code of Ethics

—— ♦ ——

The American Counseling Association (ACA) is an educational, scientific, and professional organization whose members are dedicated to the enhancement of human development throughout the life span. Association members recognize diversity in our society and embrace a cross-cultural approach in support of the worth, dignity, potential, and uniqueness of each individual. The specification of a code of ethics enables the association to clarify to current and future members, and to those served by members, the nature of the ethical responsibilities held in common by its members. As the code of ethics of the association, this document establishes principles that define the ethical behavior of association members. All members of the American Counseling Association are required to adhere to the Code of Ethics and the Standards of Practice. The Code of Ethics will serve as the basis for processing ethical complaints initiated against members of the association.

ACA Code of Ethics (effective 1995)

Section A: The Counseling Relationship

Section B: Confidentiality

Section C: Professional Responsibility

Section D: Relationships with Other Professionals

Section E: Evaluation, Assessment, and Interpretation

Section F: Teaching, Training, and Supervision

Section G: Research and Publication

Section H: Resolving Ethical Issues

SECTION A: THE COUNSELING RELATIONSHIP

A.1. CLIENT WELFARE

a. **Primary Responsibility.** The primary responsibility of counselors is to respect the dignity and to promote the welfare of clients.

b. **Positive Growth and Development.** Counselors encourage client growth and development in ways that foster the clients' interest and welfare; counselors avoid fostering dependent counseling relationships.

c. **Counseling Plans.** Counselors and their clients work jointly in devising integrated, individual counseling plans that offer reasonable promise of success and are consistent with abilities and circumstances of clients. Counselors and clients regularly review counseling plans to ensure their continued viability and effectiveness, respecting clients' freedom of choice. (See A.3.b.)

d. **Family Involvement.** Counselors recognize that families are usually important in clients' lives and strive to enlist family understanding and involvement as a positive resource, when appropriate.

e. **Career and Employment Needs.** Counselors work with their clients in considering employment in jobs and circumstances that are consistent with the clients' overall abilities, vocational limitations, physical restrictions, general temperament, interest and aptitude patterns, social skills, education, general qualifications, and other relevant characteristics and needs. Counselors neither place nor participate in placing clients in positions that will result in damaging the interest and the welfare of clients, employers, or the public.

A.2. RESPECTING DIVERSITY

a. **Nondiscrimination.** Counselors do not condone or engage in discrimination based on age, color, culture, disability, ethnic group, gender, race, religion, sexual orientation, marital status, or socioeconomic status. (See C.5.a., C.5.b., and D.1.i.)

b. **Respecting Differences.** Counselors will actively attempt to understand the diverse cultural backgrounds of the clients with whom they work. This includes, but is not limited to, learning how the counselor's own cultural/ethnic/racial identity impacts her or his values and beliefs about the counseling process. (See E.8. and F.2.i.)

A.3. CLIENT RIGHTS

a. **Disclosure to Clients.** When counseling is initiated, and throughout the counseling process as necessary, counselors inform clients of the purposes, goals, techniques, procedures, limitations, potential risks, and benefits of services to be performed, and other pertinent information. Counselors take steps to ensure that clients understand the implications of diagnosis, the intended use of tests and reports, fees, and billing arrangements. Clients have the right to expect confidentiality and to be provided with an explanation of its limitations, including supervision and/or treatment team professionals; to obtain clear information about their case records; to participate in the ongoing counseling plans; and to refuse any recommended services and be advised of the consequences of such refusal. (See E.5.a and G.2.)

b. **Freedom of Choice.** Counselors offer clients the freedom to choose whether to enter into a counseling relationship and to determine which professional(s) will provide counseling. Restrictions that limit choices of clients are fully explained. (See A.i.e.)

c. **Inability to Give Consent.** When counseling minors or persons unable to give voluntary informed consent, counselors act in these clients' best interests. (See B.3.)

A.4. CLIENTS SERVED BY OTHERS

If a client is receiving services from another mental health professional, counselors, with client consent, inform the professional persons already involved and develop clear agreements to avoid confusion and conflict for the client. (See C.6.c.)

A.5. PERSONAL NEEDS AND VALUES

a. Personal Needs. In the counseling relationship, counselors are aware of the intimacy and responsibilities inherent in the counseling relationship, maintain respect for clients, and avoid actions that seek to meet their personal needs at the expense of clients.

b. Personal Values. (Then Counselors Are Aware.) Counselors are aware of their own values, attitudes, beliefs, and behaviors and how these apply in a diverse society, and avoid imposing their values on clients. (See C.5.a.)

A.6. DUAL RELATIONSHIPS

a. Avoid When Possible. Counselors are aware of their influential positions with respect to clients, and they avoid exploiting the trust and dependency of clients. Counselors make every effort to avoid dual relationships with clients that could impair professional judgment or increase the risk of harm to clients. (Examples of such relationships include, but are not limited to, familial, social, financial, business, or close personal relationships with clients.) When a dual relationship cannot be avoided, counselors take appropriate professional precautions such as informed consent, consultation, supervision, and documentation to ensure that judgment is not impaired and no exploitation occurs. (See F.1.b.)

b. Superior/Subordinate Relationships. Counselors do not accept as clients superiors or subordinates with whom they have administrative, supervisory, or evaluative relationships.

A.7. SEXUAL INTIMACIES WITH CLIENTS

a. Current Clients. Counselors do not have any type of sexual intimacies with clients and do not counsel persons with whom they have had a sexual relationship.

b. Former Clients. Counselors do not engage in sexual intimacies with former clients within a minimum of 2 years after terminating the counseling relationship. Counselors who engage in such relationship after 2 years following termination have the responsibility to examine and document thoroughly that such relations did not have an exploitative nature, based on factors such as duration of counseling, amount of time since counseling, termination circumstances, client's personal history and mental status, adverse impact on the client, and actions by the counselor suggesting a plan to initiate a sexual relationship with the client after termination.

A.8. MULTIPLE CLIENTS

When counselors agree to provide counseling services to two or more persons who have a relationship (such as husband and wife, or parents and children), counselors clarify at the outset which person or persons are clients and the nature of the relationships they will have with each involved person. If it becomes apparent that counselors may be called upon to perform potentially conflicting roles, they clarify, adjust, or withdraw from roles appropriately. (See B.2 and B.4.d.)

A.9. GROUP WORK

a. **Screening.** Counselors screen prospective group counseling/therapy participants. To the extent possible, counselors select members whose needs and goals are compatible with goals of the group, who will not impede the group process, and whose well-being will not be jeopardized by the group experience.

b. **Protecting Clients.** In a group setting, counselors take reasonable precautions to protect clients from physical or psychological trauma.

A.10. FEES AND BARTERING (SEE D.3.A AND D.3.B.)

a. **Advance Understanding.** Counselors clearly explain to clients, prior to entering the counseling relationship, all financial arrangements related to professional services including the use of collection agencies or legal measures for nonpayment (A.11.c).

b. **Establishing Fees.** In establishing fees for professional counseling services, counselors consider the financial status of clients and locality. In the event that the established fee structure is inappropriate for a client, assistance is provided in attempting to find comparable services of acceptable cost. (See A.10.d, D.3.a, and D.3.b.)

c. **Bartering Discouraged.** Counselors ordinarily refrain from accepting goods or services from clients in return for counseling services because such arrangements create inherent potential for conflicts, exploitation, and distortion of the professional relationship. Counselors may participate in bartering only if the relationship is not exploitative, if the client requests it, if a clear written contract is established, and if such arrangements are an accepted practice among professionals in the community. (See A.6.a.)

d. **Pro Bono Service.** Counselors contribute to society by devoting a portion of their professional activity to services for which there is little or no financial return (pro bono).

A.11. TERMINATION AND REFERRAL

a. **Abandonment Prohibited.** Counselors do not abandon or neglect clients in counseling. Counselors assist in making appropriate arrangements for the continuation of treatment, when necessary, during interruptions such as vacations, and following termination.

b. **Inability to Assist Clients.** If counselors determine an inability to be of professional assistance to clients, they avoid entering or immediately terminate a counseling relationship. Counselors are knowledgeable about referral resources and suggest appropriate alternatives. If clients decline the suggested referral, counselors should discontinue the relationship.

c. **Appropriate Termination.** Counselors terminate a counseling relationship, securing client agreement when possible, when it is reasonably clear that the client is no longer benefiting, when services are no longer required, when counseling no longer serves the client's needs or interests, when clients do not pay fees charged, or when agency or institution limits do not allow provision of further counseling services. (See A.10.b and C.2.g.)

A.12. COMPUTER TECHNOLOGY

a. **Use of Computers.** When computer applications are used in counseling services, counselors ensure that (1) the client is intellectually, emotionally, and physically capable of using the computer application;

(2) the computer application is appropriate for the needs of the client; (3) the client understands the purpose and operation of the computer applications; and (4) a follow-up of client use of a computer application is provided to correct possible misconceptions, discover inappropriate use, and assess subsequent needs.

b. **Explanation of Limitations.** Counselors ensure that clients are provided information as a part of the counseling relationship that adequately explains the limitations of computer technology.

c. **Access to Computer Applications.** Counselors provide for equal access to computer applications in counseling services. (See A.2.a.)

SECTION B: CONFIDENTIALITY

B.1. RIGHT TO PRIVACY

a. **Respect for Privacy.** Counselors respect their clients' right to privacy and avoid illegal and unwarranted disclosures of confidential information. (See A.3.a and B.6.a.)

b. **Client Waiver.** The right to privacy may be waived by the client or his or her legally recognized representative.

c. **Exceptions.** The general requirement that counselors keep information confidential does not apply when disclosure is required to prevent clear and imminent danger to the client or others or when legal requirements demand that confidential information be revealed. Counselors consult with other professionals when in doubt as to the validity of an exception.

d. **Contagious, Fatal Diseases.** A counselor who receives information confirming that a client has a disease commonly known to be both communicable and fatal is justified in disclosing information to an identifiable third party, who by his or her relationship with the client is at a high risk of contracting the disease. Prior to making a disclosure the counselor should ascertain that the client has not already informed the third party about his or her disease and that the client is not intending to inform the third party in the immediate future. (See B.1.c and B.1.f.)

e. **Court-Ordered Disclosure.** When court ordered to release confidential information without a client's permission, counselors request to the court that the disclosure not be required due to potential harm to the client or counseling relationship. (See B.1.c.)

f. **Minimal Disclosure.** When circumstances require the disclosure of confidential information, only essential information is revealed. To the extent possible, clients are informed before confidential information is disclosed.

g. **Explanation of Limitations.** When counseling is initiated and throughout the counseling process as necessary, counselors inform clients of the limitations of confidentiality and identify foreseeable situations in which confidentiality must be breached. (See G.2.a.)

h. **Subordinates.** Counselors make every effort to ensure that privacy and confidentiality of clients are maintained by subordinates including employees, supervisees, clerical assistants, and volunteers. (See B.1.a.)

i. **Treatment Teams.** If client treatment will involve a continued review by a treatment team, the client will be informed of the team's existence and composition.

B.2. GROUPS AND FAMILIES

a. **Group Work.** In group work, counselors clearly define confidentiality and the parameters for the specific group being entered, explain its importance, and discuss the difficulties related to confidentiality involved in group work. The fact that confidentiality cannot be guaranteed is clearly communicated to group members.

b. **Family Counseling.** In family counseling, information about one family member cannot be disclosed to another member without permission. Counselors protect the privacy rights of each family member. (See A.8, B.3, and B.4.d.)

B.3. MINOR OR INCOMPETENT CLIENTS

When counseling clients who are minors or individuals who are unable to give voluntary, informed consent, parents or guardians may be included in the counseling process as appropriate. Counselors act in the best interests of clients and take measures to safeguard confidentiality. (See A.3.c.)

B.4. RECORDS

a. Requirement of Records. Counselors maintain records necessary for rendering professional services to their clients and as required by laws, regulations, or agency or institution procedures.

b. Confidentiality of Records. Counselors are responsible for securing the safety and confidentiality of any counseling records they create, maintain, transfer, or destroy whether the records are written, taped, computerized, or stored in any other medium. (See B.1.a.)

c. Permission to Record or Observe. Counselors obtain permission from clients prior to electronically recording or observing sessions. (See A.3.a.)

d. Client Access. Counselors recognize that counseling records are kept for the benefit of clients, and therefore provide access to records and copies of records when requested by competent clients, unless the records contain information that may be misleading and detrimental to the client. In situations involving multiple clients, access to records is limited to those parts of records that do not include confidential information related to another client. (See A.8, B.1.a, and B.2.b.)

e. Disclosure or Transfer. Counselors obtain written permission from clients to disclose or transfer records to legitimate third parties unless exceptions to confidentiality exist as listed in Section B.1. Steps are taken to ensure that receivers of counseling records are sensitive to their confidential nature.

B.5. RESEARCH AND TRAINING

a. Data Disguise Required. Use of data derived from counseling relationships for purposes of training, research, or publication is confined to content that is disguised to ensure the anonymity of the individuals involved. (See B.1.g and G.3.d.)

b. Agreement for Identification. Identification of a client in a presentation or publication is permissible only when the client has reviewed the material and has agreed to its presentation or publication. (See G.3.d.)

B.6. CONSULTATION

a. **Respect for Privacy.** Information obtained in a consulting relationship is discussed for professional purposes only with persons clearly concerned with the case. Written and oral reports present data germane to the purposes of the consultation, and every effort is made to protect client identity and avoid undue invasion of privacy.

b. **Cooperating Agencies.** Before sharing information, counselors make efforts to ensure that there are defined policies in other agencies serving the counselor's clients that effectively protect the confidentiality of information.

SECTION C: PROFESSIONAL RESPONSIBILITY

C.1. STANDARDS KNOWLEDGE

Counselors have a responsibility to read, understand, and follow the Code of Ethics and the Standards of Practice.

C.2. PROFESSIONAL COMPETENCE

a. **Boundaries of Competence.** Counselors practice only within the boundaries of their competence, based on their education, training, supervised experience, state and national professional credentials, and appropriate professional experience. Counselors will demonstrate a commitment to gain knowledge, personal awareness, sensitivity, and skills pertinent to working with a diverse client population.

b. **New Specialty Areas of Practice.** Counselors practice in specialty areas new to them only after appropriate education, training, and supervised experience. While developing skills in new specialty areas, counselors take steps to ensure the competence of their work and to protect others from possible harm.

c. **Qualified for Employment.** Counselors accept employment only for positions for which they are qualified by education, training, supervised experience, state and national professional credentials, and appropriate professional experience. Counselors hire for professional counseling positions only individuals who are qualified and competent.

d. **Monitor Effectiveness.** Counselors continually monitor their effectiveness as professionals and take steps to improve when necessary. Counselors in private practice take reasonable steps to seek out peer supervision to evaluate their efficacy as counselors.

e. **Ethical Issues Consultation.** Counselors take reasonable steps to consult with other counselors or related professionals when they have questions regarding their ethical obligations or professional practice. (See H.1.)

f. **Continuing Education.** Counselors recognize the need for continuing education to maintain a reasonable level of awareness of current scientific and professional information in their fields of activity. They take steps to maintain competence in the skills they use, are open to new procedures, and keep current with the diverse and/or special populations with whom they work.

g. **Impairment.** Counselors refrain from offering or accepting professional services when their physical, mental, or emotional problems are likely to harm a client or others. They are alert to the signs of impairment, seek assistance for problems, and, if necessary, limit, suspend, or terminate their professional responsibilities. (See A.11.c.)

C.3. ADVERTISING AND SOLICITING CLIENTS

a. **Accurate Advertising.** There are no restrictions on advertising by counselors except those that can be specifically justified to protect the public from deceptive practices. Counselors advertise or represent their services to the public by identifying their credentials in an accurate manner that is not false, misleading, deceptive, or fraudulent. Counselors may only advertise the highest degree earned which is in counseling or a closely related field from a college or university that was accredited when the degree was awarded by one of the regional accrediting bodies recognized by the Council on Postsecondary Accreditation.

b. **Testimonials.** Counselors who use testimonials do not solicit them from clients or other persons who, because of their particular circumstances, may be vulnerable to undue influence.

c. **Statements by Others.** Counselors make reasonable efforts to ensure that statements made by others about them or the profession of counseling are accurate.

d. **Recruiting Through Employment.** Counselors do not use their places of employment or institutional affiliation to recruit or gain clients, supervisees, or consultees for their private practices. (See C.5.e.)

e. **Products and Training Advertisements.** Counselors who develop products related to their profession or conduct workshops or training events ensure that the advertisements concerning these products or events are accurate and disclose adequate information for consumers to make informed choices.

f. **Promoting to Those Served.** Counselors do not use counseling, teaching, training, or supervisory relationships to promote their products or training events in a manner that is deceptive or would exert undue influence on individuals who may be vulnerable. Counselors may adopt textbooks they have authored for instruction purposes.

g. **Professional Association Involvement.** Counselors actively participate in local, state, and national associations that foster the development and improvement of counseling.

C.4. CREDENTIALS

a. **Credentials Claimed.** Counselors claim or imply only professional credentials possessed and are responsible for correcting any known misrepresentations of their credentials by others. Professional credentials include graduate degrees in counseling or closely related mental health fields, accreditation of graduate programs, national voluntary certifications, government-issued certifications or licenses, ACA professional membership, or any other credential that might indicate to the public specialized knowledge or expertise in counseling.

b. **ACA Professional Membership.** ACA professional members may announce to the public their membership status. Regular members may not announce their ACA membership in a manner that might imply they are credentialed counselors.

c. **Credential Guidelines.** Counselors follow the guidelines for use of credentials that have been established by the entities that issue the credentials.

d. **Misrepresentation of Credentials.** Counselors do not attribute more to their credentials than the credentials represent, and do not imply that other counselors are not qualified because they do not possess certain credentials.

e. **Doctoral Degrees From Other Fields.** Counselors who hold a master's degree in counseling or a closely related mental health field, but hold a doctoral degree from other than counseling or a closely related field, do not use the title "Dr." in their practices and do not announce to the public in relation to their practice or status as a counselor that they hold a doctorate.

C.5. PUBLIC RESPONSIBILITY

a. **Nondiscrimination.** Counselors do not discriminate against clients, students, or supervisees in a manner that has a negative impact based on their age, color, culture, disability, ethnic group, gender, race, religion, sexual orientation, or socioeconomic status, or for any other reason. (See A.2.a.)

b. **Sexual Harassment.** Counselors do not engage in sexual harassment. Sexual harassment is defined as sexual solicitation, physical advances, or verbal or nonverbal conduct that is sexual in nature, that occurs in connection with professional activities or roles, and that either (1) is unwelcome, is offensive, or creates a hostile workplace environment, and counselors know or are told this; or (2) is sufficiently severe or intense to be perceived as harassment to a reasonable person in the context. Sexual harassment can consist of a single intense or severe act or multiple persistent or pervasive acts.

c. **Reports to Third Parties.** Counselors are accurate, honest, and unbiased in reporting their professional activities and judgments to appropriate third parties including courts, health insurance companies, those who are the recipients of evaluation reports, and others. (See B.1.g.)

d. **Media Presentations.** When counselors provide advice or comment by means of public lectures, demonstrations, radio or television programs, prerecorded tapes, printed articles, mailed material, or other media, they take reasonable precautions to ensure that (1) the statements are based on appropriate professional counseling literature and practice; (2) the statements are otherwise consistent with the Code of Ethics and the Standards of Practice; and (3) the recipients of the information are not encouraged to infer that a professional counseling relationship has been established. (See C.6.b.)

e. **Unjustified Gains.** Counselors do not use their professional positions to seek or receive unjustified personal gains, sexual favors, unfair advantage, or unearned goods or services. (See C.3.d.)

C.6. RESPONSIBILITY TO OTHER PROFESSIONALS

a. **Different Approaches.** Counselors are respectful of approaches to professional counseling that differ from their own. Counselors know and take into account the traditions and practices of other professional groups with which they work.

b. **Personal Public Statements.** When making personal statements in a public context, counselors clarify that they are speaking from their personal perspectives and that they are not speaking on behalf of all counselors or the profession. (See C.5.d.)

c. **Clients Served by Others.** When counselors learn that their clients are in a professional relationship with another mental health professional, they request release from clients to inform the other professionals and strive to establish positive and collaborative professional relationships. (See A.4.)

SECTION D: RELATIONSHIPS WITH OTHER PROFESSIONALS

D.1. RELATIONSHIPS WITH EMPLOYERS AND EMPLOYEES

a. **Role Definition.** Counselors define and describe for their employers and employees the parameters and levels of their professional roles.

b. **Agreements.** Counselors establish working agreements with supervisors, colleagues, and subordinates regarding counseling or clinical relationships, confidentiality, adherence to professional standards, distinction between public and private material, maintenance and dissemination of recorded information, work load, and accountability. Working agreements in each instance are specified and made known to those concerned.

c. **Negative Conditions.** Counselors alert their employers to conditions that may be potentially disruptive or damaging to the counselor's professional responsibilities or that may limit their effectiveness.

d. **Evaluation.** Counselors submit regularly to professional review and evaluation by their supervisor or the appropriate representative of the employer.

e. **In-Service.** Counselors are responsible for in-service development of self and staff.

f. **Goals.** Counselors inform their staff of goals and programs.

g. **Practices.** Counselors provide personnel and agency practices that respect and enhance the rights and welfare of each employee and recipient of agency services. Counselors strive to maintain the highest levels of professional services.

h. **Personnel Selection and Assignment.** Counselors select competent staff and assign responsibilities compatible with their skills and experiences.

i. **Discrimination.** Counselors, as either employers or employees, do not engage in or condone practices that are inhumane, illegal, or unjustifiable (such as considerations based on age, color, culture, disability, ethnic group, gender, race, religion, sexual orientation, or socioeconomic status) in hiring, promotion, or training. (See A.2.a and C.5.b.)

j. **Professional Conduct.** Counselors have a responsibility both to clients and to the agency or institution within which services are performed to maintain high standards of professional conduct.

k. **Exploitative Relationships.** Counselors do not engage in exploitative relationships with individuals over whom they have supervisory, evaluative, or instructional control or authority.

l. **Employer Policies.** The acceptance of employment in an agency or institution implies that counselors are in agreement with its general policies and principles. Counselors strive to reach agreement with employers as to acceptable standards of conduct that allow for changes in institutional policy conducive to the growth and development of clients.

D.2. CONSULTATION (SEE B.6.)

a. **Consultation as an Option.** Counselors may choose to consult with any other professionally competent persons about their clients. In choosing consultants, counselors avoid placing the consultant in a conflict of interest situation that would preclude the consultant being a proper party to the counselor's efforts to help the client. Should counselors be engaged in a work setting that compromises this consultation standard, they consult with other professionals whenever possible to consider justifiable alternatives.

b. **Consultant Competency.** Counselors are reasonably certain that they have or the organization represented has the necessary competencies and resources for giving the kind of consulting services needed and that appropriate referral resources are available.

c. **Understanding with Clients.** When providing consultation, counselors attempt to develop with their clients a clear understanding of problem definition, goals for change, and predicted consequences of interventions selected.

d. **Consultant Goals.** The consulting relationship is one in which client adaptability and growth toward self-direction are consistently encouraged and cultivated. (See A.1.b.)

D.3. FEES FOR REFERRAL

a. **Accepting Fees from Agency Clients.** Counselors refuse a private fee or other remuneration for rendering services to persons who are entitled to such services through the counselor's employing agency or institution. The policies of a particular agency may make explicit provisions for agency clients to receive counseling services from members of its staff in private practice. In such instances, the clients must be informed of other options open to them should they seek private counseling services. (See A.10.a, A.11.b, and C.3.d.)

b. **Referral Fees.** Counselors do not accept a referral fee from other professionals.

D.4. SUBCONTRACTOR ARRANGEMENTS

When counselors work as subcontractors for counseling services for a third party, they have a duty to inform clients of the limitations of confidentiality that the organization may place on counselors in providing counseling services to clients. The limits of such confidentiality ordinarily are discussed as part of the intake session. (See B.1.e and B.1.f.)

SECTION E: EVALUATION, ASSESSMENT, AND INTERPRETATION

E.1. GENERAL

a. **Appraisal Techniques.** The primary purpose of educational and psychological assessment is to provide measures that are objective and interpretable in either comparative or absolute terms. Counselors recognize the need to interpret the statements in this section as applying to the whole range of appraisal techniques, including test and nontest data.

b. **Client Welfare.** Counselors promote the welfare and best interests of the client in the development, publication, and utilization of educational and psychological assessment techniques. They do not misuse assessment results and interpretations and take reasonable steps to prevent others from misusing the information these techniques provide. They respect the client's right to know the results, the interpretations made, and the bases for their conclusions and recommendations.

E.2. COMPETENCE TO USE AND INTERPRET TESTS

a. **Limits of Competence.** Counselors recognize the limits of their competence and perform only those testing and assessment services for which they have been trained. They are familiar with reliability, validity, related standardization, error of measurement, and proper application of any technique utilized. Counselors using computer-based test interpretations are trained in the construct being measured and the specific instrument being used prior to using this type of computer application. Counselors take reasonable measures to ensure the proper use of psychological assessment techniques by persons under their supervision.

b. **Appropriate Use.** Counselors are responsible for the appropriate application, scoring, interpretation, and use of assessment instruments, whether they score and interpret such tests themselves or use computerized or other services.

c. **Decisions Based on Results.** Counselors responsible for decisions involving individuals or policies that are based on assessment results have a thorough understanding of educational and psychological measurement, including validation criteria, test research, and guidelines for test development and use.

d. **Accurate Information.** Counselors provide accurate information and avoid false claims or misconceptions when making statements about assessment instruments or techniques. Special efforts are made to avoid unwarranted connotations of such terms as IQ and grade equivalent scores. (See C.5.c.)

E.3. INFORMED CONSENT

a. **Explanation to Clients.** Prior to assessment, counselors explain the nature and purposes of assessment and the specific use of results in language the client (or other legally authorized person on behalf of the client) can understand, unless an explicit exception to this right has been agreed upon in advance. Regardless of whether scoring and interpretation are completed by counselors, by assistants, or by computer or other outside services, counselors take reasonable steps to ensure that appropriate explanations are given to the client.

b. **Recipients of Results.** The examinee's welfare, explicit understanding, and prior agreement determine the recipients of test results. Counselors include accurate and appropriate interpretations with any release of individual or group test results. (See B.1.a and C.5.c.)

E.4. RELEASE OF INFORMATION TO COMPETENT PROFESSIONALS

a. **Misuse of Results.** Counselors do not misuse assessment results, including test results, and interpretations, and take reasonable steps to prevent the misuse of such by others. (See C.5.c.)

b. **Release of Raw Data.** Counselors ordinarily release data (e.g., protocols, counseling or interview notes, or questionnaires) in which the client is identified only with the consent of the client or the client's legal representative. Such data are usually released only to persons recognized by counselors as competent to interpret the data. (See B.1.a.)

E.5. PROPER DIAGNOSIS OF MENTAL DISORDERS

a. **Proper Diagnosis.** Counselors take special care to provide proper diagnosis of mental disorders. Assessment techniques (including personal interview) used to determine client care (e.g., locus of treatment, type of treatment, or recommended follow-up) are carefully selected and appropriately used. (See A.3.a and C.5.c.)

b. **Cultural Sensitivity.** Counselors recognize that culture affects the manner in which clients' problems are defined. Clients' socioeconomic and cultural experience is considered when diagnosing mental disorders.

E.6. TEST SELECTION

a. **Appropriateness of Instruments.** Counselors carefully consider the validity, reliability, psychometric limitations, and appropriateness of instruments when selecting tests for use in a given situation or with a particular client.

b. **Culturally Diverse Populations.** Counselors are cautious when selecting tests for culturally diverse populations to avoid inappropriateness of testing that may be outside of socialized behavioral or cognitive patterns.

E.7. CONDITIONS OF TEST ADMINISTRATION

a. **Administration Conditions.** Counselors administer tests under the same conditions that were established in their standardization. When tests are not administered under standard conditions or when unusual behavior or irregularities occur during the testing session, those conditions are noted in interpretation, and the results may be designated as invalid or of questionable validity.

b. **Computer Administration.** Counselors are responsible for ensuring that administration programs function properly to provide clients with accurate results when a computer or other electronic methods are used for test administration. (See A.12.b.)

c. **Unsupervised Test Taking.** Counselors do not permit unsupervised or inadequately supervised use of tests or assessments unless the tests or assessments are designed, intended, and validated for self-administration and/or scoring.

d. **Disclosure of Favorable Conditions.** Prior to test administration, conditions that produce most favorable test results are made known to the examinee.

E.8. DIVERSITY IN TESTING

Counselors are cautious in using assessment techniques, making evaluations, and interpreting the performance of populations not represented in the norm group on which an instrument was standardized. They recognize the effects of age, color, culture, disability, ethnic group, gender, race, religion, sexual orientation, and socioeconomic status on test administration and interpretation and place test results in proper perspective with other relevant factors. (See A.2.a.)

E.9. TEST SCORING AND INTERPRETATION

a. **Reporting Reservations.** In reporting assessment results, counselors indicate any reservations that exist regarding validity or reliability because of the circumstances of the assessment or the inappropriateness of the norms for the person tested.

b. **Research Instruments.** Counselors exercise caution when interpreting the results of research instruments possessing insufficient technical data to support respondent results. The specific purposes for the use of such instruments are stated explicitly to the examinee.

c. **Testing Services.** Counselors who provide test scoring and test interpretation services to support the assessment process confirm the validity of such interpretations. They accurately describe the purpose, norms, validity, reliability, and applications of the procedures and any special qualifications applicable to their use. The public offering of an automated test interpretations service is considered a professional-to-professional consultation. The formal responsibility of the consultant is to the consultee, but the ultimate and overriding responsibility is to the client.

E.10. TEST SECURITY

Counselors maintain the integrity and security of tests and other assessment techniques consistent with legal and contractual obligations. Counselors do not appropriate, reproduce, or modify published tests or parts thereof without acknowledgment and permission from the publisher.

E.11. OBSOLETE TESTS AND OUTDATED TEST RESULTS

Counselors do not use data or test results that are obsolete or outdated for the current purpose. Counselors make every effort to prevent the misuse of obsolete measures and test data by others.

E.12. TEST CONSTRUCTION

Counselors use established scientific procedures, relevant standards, and current professional knowledge for test design in the development, publication, and utilization of educational and psychological assessment techniques.

SECTION F: TEACHING, TRAINING, AND SUPERVISION

F.1. COUNSELOR EDUCATORS AND TRAINERS

a. **Educators as Teachers and Practitioners.** Counselors who are responsible for developing, implementing, and supervising educational programs are skilled as teachers and practitioners. They are knowledgeable regarding the ethical, legal, and regulatory aspects of the profession, are skilled in applying that knowledge, and make students and supervisees aware of their responsibilities. Counselors conduct counselor education and training programs in an ethical manner and serve as role models for professional behavior. Counselor educators should make an effort to infuse material related to human diversity into all courses and/or workshops that are designed to promote the development of professional counselors.

b. **Relationship Boundaries with Students and Supervisees.** Counselors clearly define and maintain ethical, professional, and social relationship boundaries with their students and supervisees. They are aware of the differential in power that exists and the students or supervisee's possible incomprehension of that power differential. Counselors explain to students and supervisees the potential for the relationship to become exploitive.

c. **Sexual Relationships.** Counselors do not engage in sexual relationships with students or supervisees and do not subject them to sexual harassment. (See A.6 and C.5.b.)

d. **Contributions to Research.** Counselors give credit to students or supervisees for their contributions to research and scholarly projects. Credit is given through coauthorship, acknowledgment, footnote statement, or other appropriate means, in accordance with such contributions. (See G.4.b and G.4.c.)

e. **Close Relatives.** Counselors do not accept close relatives as students or supervisees.

f. Supervision Preparation. Counselors who offer clinical supervision services are adequately prepared in supervision methods and techniques. Counselors who are doctoral students serving as practicum or internship supervisors to master's level students are adequately prepared and supervised by the training program.

g. Responsibility for Services to Clients. Counselors who supervise the counseling services of others take reasonable measures to ensure that counseling services provided to clients are professional.

h. Endorsement. Counselors do not endorse students or supervisees for certification, licensure, employment, or completion of an academic or training program if they believe students or supervisees are not qualified for the endorsement. Counselors take reasonable steps to assist students or supervisees who are not qualified for endorsement to become qualified.

F.2. COUNSELOR EDUCATION AND TRAINING PROGRAMS

a. Orientation. Prior to admission, counselors orient prospective students to the counselor education or training program's expectations, including but not limited to the following: (1) the type and level of skill acquisition required for successful completion of the training, (2) subject matter to be covered, (3) basis for evaluation, (4) training components that encourage self-growth or self-disclosure as part of the training process, (5) the type of supervision settings and requirements of the sites for required clinical field experiences, (6) student and supervisee evaluation and dismissal policies and procedures, and (7) up-to-date employment prospects for graduates.

b. Integration of Study and Practice. Counselors establish counselor education and training programs that integrate academic study and supervised practice.

c. Evaluation. Counselors clearly state to students and supervisees, in advance of training, the levels of competency expected, appraisal methods, and timing of evaluations for both didactic and experiential components. Counselors provide students and supervisees with periodic performance appraisal and evaluation feedback throughout the training program.

d. Teaching Ethics. Counselors make students and supervisees aware of the ethical responsibilities and standards of the profession and the students' and supervisees' ethical responsibilities to the profession. (See C.1 and F.3.e.)

e. **Peer Relationships.** When students or supervisees are assigned to lead counseling groups or provide clinical supervision for their peers, counselors take steps to ensure that students and supervisees placed in these roles do not have personal or adverse relationships with peers and that they understand they have the same ethical obligations as counselor educators, trainers, and supervisors. Counselors make every effort to ensure that the rights of peers are not compromised when students or supervisees are assigned to lead counseling groups or provide clinical supervision.

f. **Varied Theoretical Positions.** Counselors present varied theoretical positions so that students and supervisees may make comparisons and have opportunities to develop their own positions. Counselors provide information concerning the scientific bases of professional practice. (See C.6.a.)

g. **Field Placements.** Counselors develop clear policies within their training program regarding field placement and other clinical experiences. Counselors provide clearly stated roles and responsibilities for the student or supervisee, the site supervisor, and the program supervisor. They confirm that site supervisors are qualified to provide supervision and are informed of their professional and ethical responsibilities in this role.

h. **Dual Relationships as Supervisors.** Counselors avoid dual relationships such as performing the role of site supervisor and training program supervisor in the student's or supervisee's training program. Counselors do not accept any form of professional services, fees, commissions, reimbursement, or remuneration from a site for student or supervisee placement.

i. **Diversity in Programs.** Counselors are responsive to their institution's and program's recruitment and retention needs for training program administrators, faculty, and students with diverse backgrounds and special needs. (See A.2.a.)

F.3. STUDENTS AND SUPERVISEES

a. **Limitations.** Counselors, through ongoing evaluation and appraisal, are aware of the academic and personal limitations of students and supervisees that might impede performance. Counselors assist students and supervisees in securing remedial assistance when needed, and dismiss from the training program supervisees who are unable to provide competent service due to academic or personal limitations. Counselors seek professional consultation and document their decision to dismiss or refer students or supervisees for assistance. Counselors ensure that students and supervisees have recourse to address decisions made to require them to seek assistance or to dismiss them.

b. **Self-Growth Experiences.** Counselors use professional judgment when designing training experiences conducted by the counselors themselves that require student and supervisee self-growth or self-disclosure. Safeguards are provided so that students and supervisees are aware of the ramifications their self-disclosure may have on counselors whose primary role as teacher, trainer, or supervisor requires acting on ethical obligations to the profession. Evaluative components of experiential training experiences explicitly delineate predetermined academic standards that are separate and do not depend on the student's level of self-disclosure. (See A.6.)

c. **Counseling for Students and Supervisees.** If students or supervisees request counseling, supervisors or counselor educators provide them with acceptable referrals. Supervisors or counselor educators do not serve as counselor to students or supervisees over whom they hold administrative, teaching, or evaluative roles unless this is a brief role associated with a training experience. (See A.6.b.)

d. **Clients of Students and Supervisees.** Counselors make every effort to ensure that the clients at field placements are aware of the services rendered and the qualifications of the students and supervisees rendering those services. Clients receive professional disclosure information and are informed of the limits of confidentiality. Client permission is obtained in order for the students and supervisees to use any information concerning the counseling relationship in the training process. (See B.1.e.)

e. **Standards for Students and Supervisees.** Students and supervisees preparing to become counselors adhere to the Code of Ethics and the Standards of Practice. Students and supervisees have the same obligations to clients as those required of counselors. (See H.1.)

SECTION G: RESEARCH AND PUBLICATION

G.1. RESEARCH RESPONSIBILITIES

a. **Use of Human Subjects.** Counselors plan, design, conduct, and report research in a manner consistent with pertinent ethical principles, federal and state laws, host institutional regulations, and scientific standards governing research with human subjects. Counselors design and conduct research that reflects cultural sensitivity appropriateness.

b. Deviation from Standard Practices. Counselors seek consultation and observe stringent safeguards to protect the rights of research participants when a research problem suggests a deviation from standard acceptable practices. (See B.6.)

c. Precautions to Avoid Injury. Counselors who conduct research with human subjects are responsible for the subjects' welfare throughout the experiment and take reasonable precautions to avoid causing injurious psychological, physical, or social effects to their subjects.

d. Principal Researcher Responsibility. The ultimate responsibility for ethical research practice lies with the principal researcher. All others involved in the research activities share ethical obligations and full responsibility for their own actions.

e. Minimal Interference. Counselors take reasonable precautions to avoid causing disruptions in subjects' lives due to participation in research.

f. Diversity. Counselors are sensitive to diversity and research issues with special populations. They seek consultation when appropriate. (See A.2.a and B.6.)

G.2. INFORMED CONSENT

a. Topics Disclosed. In obtaining informed consent for research, counselors use language that is understandable to research participants and that (1) accurately explains the purpose and procedures to be followed; (2) identifies any procedures that are experimental or relatively untried; (3) describes the attendant discomforts and risks; (4) describes the benefits or changes in individuals or organizations that might be reasonably expected; (5) discloses appropriate alternative procedures that would be advantageous for subjects; (6) offers to answer any inquiries concerning the procedures; (7) describes any limitations on confidentiality; and (8) instructs that subjects are free to withdraw their consent and to discontinue participation in the project at any time. (See B.1.f.)

b. Deception. Counselors do not conduct research involving deception unless alternative procedures are not feasible and the prospective value of the research justifies the deception. When the methodological requirements of a study necessitate concealment or deception, the investigator is required to explain clearly the reasons for this action as soon as possible.

c. **Voluntary Participation.** Participation in research is typically voluntary and without any penalty for refusal to participate. Involuntary participation is appropriate only when it can be demonstrated that participation will have no harmful effects on subjects and is essential to the investigation.

d. **Confidentiality of Information.** Information obtained about research participants during the course of an investigation is confidential. When the possibility exists that others may obtain access to such information, ethical research practice requires that the possibility, together with the plans for protecting confidentiality, be explained to participants as a part of the procedure for obtaining informed consent. (See B.1.e.)

e. **Persons Incapable of Giving Informed Consent.** When a person is incapable of giving informed consent, counselors provide an appropriate explanation, obtain agreement for participation, and obtain appropriate consent from a legally authorized person.

f. **Commitments to Participants.** Counselors take reasonable measures to honor all commitments to research participants.

g. **Explanations after Data Collection.** After data are collected, counselors provide participants with full clarification of the nature of the study to remove any misconceptions. Where scientific or human values justify delaying or withholding information, counselors take reasonable measures to avoid causing harm.

h. **Agreements to Cooperate.** Counselors who agree to cooperate with another individual in research or publication incur an obligation to cooperate as promised in terms of punctuality of performance and with regard to the completeness and accuracy of the information required.

i. **Informed Consent for Sponsors.** In the pursuit of research, counselors give sponsors, institutions, and publication channels the same respect and opportunity for giving informed consent that they accord to individual research participants. Counselors are aware of their obligation to future research workers and ensure that host institutions are given feedback information and proper acknowledgment.

G.3. REPORTING RESULTS

a. **Information Affecting Outcome.** When reporting research results, counselors explicitly mention all variables and conditions known to the investigator that may have affected the outcome of a study or the interpretation of data.

b. **Accurate Results.** Counselors plan, conduct, and report research accurately and in a manner that minimizes the possibility that results will be misleading. They provide thorough discussions of the limitations of their data and alternative hypotheses. Counselors do not engage in fraudulent research, distort data, misrepresent data, or deliberately bias their results.

c. **Obligation to Report Unfavorable Results.** Counselors communicate to other counselors the results of any research judged to be of professional value. Results that reflect unfavorably on institutions, programs, services, prevailing opinions, or vested interests are not withheld.

d. **Identity of Subjects.** Counselors who supply data, aid in the research of another person, report research results, or make original data available take due care to disguise the identity of respective subjects in the absence of specific authorization from the subjects to do otherwise. (See B.1.g and B.5.a.)

e. **Replication Studies.** Counselors are obligated to make available sufficient original research data to qualified professionals who may wish to replicate the study.

G.4. PUBLICATION

a. **Recognition of Others.** When conducting and reporting research, counselors are familiar with and give recognition to previous work on the topic, observe copyright laws, and give full credit to those to whom credit is due. (See F.1.d and G.4.c.)

b. **Contributors.** Counselors give credit through joint authorship, acknowledgment, footnote statements, or other appropriate means to those who have contributed significantly to research or concept development in accordance with such contributions. The principal contributor is listed first and minor technical or professional contributions are acknowledged in notes or introductory statements.

c. **Student Research.** For an article that is substantially based on a student's dissertation or thesis, the student is listed as the principal author. (See F.1.d and G.4.a.)

d. **Duplicate Submission.** Counselors submit manuscripts for consideration to only one journal at a time. Manuscripts that are published in whole or in substantial part in another journal or published work are not submitted for publication without acknowledgment and permission from the previous publication.

e. **Professional Review.** Counselors who review material submitted for publication, research, or other scholarly purposes respect the confidentiality and proprietary rights of those who submitted it.

SECTION H: RESOLVING ETHICAL ISSUES

H.1. KNOWLEDGE OF STANDARDS

Counselors are familiar with the Code of Ethics and the Standards of Practice and other applicable ethics codes from other professional organizations of which they are member, or from certification and licensure bodies. Lack of knowledge or misunderstanding of an ethical responsibility is not a defense against a charge of unethical conduct. (See F.3.e.)

H.2. SUSPECTED VIOLATIONS

a. **Ethical Behavior Expected.** Counselors expect professional associates to adhere to the Code of Ethics. When counselors possess reasonable cause that raises doubts as to whether a counselor is acting in an ethical manner, they take appropriate action. (See H.2.d and H.2.e.)

b. **Consultation.** When uncertain as to whether a particular situation or course of action may be in violation of the Code of Ethics, counselors consult with other counselors who are knowledgeable about ethics, with colleagues, or with appropriate authorities.

c. **Organization Conflicts.** If the demands of an organization with which counselors are affiliated pose a conflict with the Code of Ethics, counselors specify the nature of such conflicts and express to their supervisors or other responsible officials their commitment to the Code of Ethics. When possible, counselors work toward change within the organization to allow full adherence to the Code of Ethics.

d. Informal Resolution. When counselors have reasonable cause to believe that another counselor is violating an ethical standard, they attempt to first resolve the issue informally with the other counselor if feasible, providing that such action does not violate confidentiality rights that may be involved.

e. Reporting Suspected Violations. When an informal resolution is not appropriate or feasible, counselors, upon reasonable cause, take action such as reporting the suspected ethical violation to state or national ethics committees, unless this action conflicts with confidentiality rights that cannot be resolved.

f. Unwarranted Complaints. Counselors do not initiate, participate in, or encourage the filing of ethics complaints that are unwarranted or intend to harm a counselor rather than to protect clients or the public.

H.3. COOPERATION WITH ETHICS COMMITTEES

Counselors assist in the process of enforcing the Code of Ethics. Counselors cooperate with investigations, proceedings, and requirements of the ACA Ethics Committee or ethics committees of other duly constituted associations or boards having jurisdiction over those charged with a violation. Counselors are familiar with the ACA Policies and Procedures and use it as a reference in assisting the enforcement of the Code of Ethics.

Appendix D

Building Consultation Skills
An Application-Learning Model

Counselors entering schools should be prepared to support the school's academic mission by promoting and enhancing the learning process (Bowers & Hatch, 2002). To accomplish this goal, counselors need the knowledge and skills that allow them to facilitate the personal/social, career, and academic growth of students through interventions with students, teachers, parents, and administrators. These interventions include individual and group counseling, classroom guidance, and consultation and are part of a balanced comprehensive developmental guidance program. Consultation, as a counselor intervention, is the focus of this text. An application-learning model is used to develop skills in two primary areas: case consultation and workshop presentation.

PREPARATION FOR CONSULTATIVE ROLE

State and national agencies that oversee counselor preparation have recognized the need for consultative skills to be well developed as large numbers of students can be impacted through work with parents, teachers, and administrators. ASCA's National Standards for School Counselors (Campbell & Dahir, 1997) reflect the shift in focus to student achievement while increasing the school counselor's collaborative role with teachers and administrators (Dahir, Sheldon, & Valiga, 1998). The Council for Accreditation of

Counseling and Related Educational Programs (CACREP, 2001) identifies knowledge and skills in consultation as part of the school counselor specialization. Bradley (1997), in his review of state departments of education across the country, identified consultation as part of the common school counselor education curriculum required for certification.

Even so, not all counselor education programs offer a separate consultation course to prepare school counselors for these consultative tasks. A recent national survey (Perusse, Goodnough, & Noel, 2001) found that only about 20% of participating school counselor preparation programs offered a separate course in consultation. We believe it is an essential component with specific skills that can be used to make a difference with students through working with the adults who are charged with their learning and development.

GOALS FOR THIS TEXT

Our goal for this text is to provide a framework for a hands-on approach to developing the knowledge and skills school counselors need to function as effective consultants in schools. A foundation is laid through the introduction of theory, consulting approaches, and their application in school settings. An increased integration of theory and practice is offered through an experiential approach to developing competence as a consultant to parents, teachers, and administrators. After reading this text, school counselors will have the knowledge, skills, and confidence to effectively deliver consultation as one of the interventions supporting increased learning opportunities for students. This appendix provides an overview of some of the techniques and strategies that have been used in course delivery as well as some sample activities used to support learning as school counselors build an ongoing base of knowledge and integrate consultative skills into their school counselor role.[1]

"TELL, SHOW, DO, COACH" MODEL

Teaching the consultative process involves building a knowledge base, and introducing the necessary skills to facilitate that process. Comprehensive

---

[1] The model discussed can be used with preservice school counselors in university programs, as well as with in-service school counselors who seek to review or enhance their consultation skills. To avoid confusion, the term *school counselor* will be used to refer to both preservice and in-service school counselors.

training in consultation includes didactic instruction, practice, and experience (Deck, 1992). This "tell, show, do, coach" model provides opportunities to learn, see skills demonstrated, practice, and receive feedback as part of the course, culminating with opportunities for school counselors to demonstrate their ability to integrate their knowledge base with initial mastery of consultative skills. This increases confidence and the likelihood that counselors will be able to effectively facilitate the consultative process in their schools.

TELL

The "tell" portion of the course begins with general information about consultation. A brief history of school consultation, an overview of the consultative process, and a differentiation between consultation and counseling help to orient school counselors to consultation in general and introduce them to issues that have ethical ramifications. Information about the different approaches to consultation is also provided.

As school counselors are demonstrating consultative skills throughout the course they can also contribute to this "tell" part of the model as they provide well researched information on topics frequently emerging during consultation. Specific topics such as child abuse, loss, violence prevention, and changing families can be addressed along with information about appropriate resources and interventions.

Kits such as *STEP* (Dinkmeyer & McKay, 1997a) and *Cooperative Discipline* (Albert, 1996) can be used to illustrate methods of group consultation with parents and teachers.

SHOW/DO

Two important skill sets to develop in this course are case consultation skills and workshop presentation skills. The process of observing these skills being used in context and practicing the skills during class speeds skill acquisition and deepens understanding. By practicing in small groups school counselors have the opportunity to see multiple models for these two important skill sets as well as several core skills such as listening, attending, providing feedback, and eliciting input and information. A structured guide is provided for both the case consultation and the workshop. This guide is incorporated into the feedback forms used by observers as shown in Tables D.1 and D.2.

Table D.1   Case Consultation Feedback Form

Graduate student's name: _____   Rater's name: _____

Date of review: _____   Focus of consultation: _____

Please rate each of the following categories:

	Lowest			*Highest*	
Before Consultation					
Evidence of PR review, information from parents, teachers	1	2	3	4	5
During Consultation					
1. Structure meeting—time, topic, process	1	2	3	4	5
2. Start with positives/strengths	1	2	3	4	5
3. Clarify problem in concrete behavioral terms including duration and frequency	1	2	3	4	5
4. Clarify goal of consultation in behavioral terms	1	2	3	4	5
5. Clarify everything that has been tried and results— include examples and child's reaction to intervention and adult's emotional reaction	1	2	3	4	5
6. Goal of student behavior identified	1	2	3	4	5
7. Clarify what client thinks might work	1	2	3	4	5
8. Gather missing information: Peer relations academic strengths/weaknesses, academic and peer performance of siblings, relationship to parents and siblings	1	2	3	4	5
9. Recommendations/suggestions offered as additional alternatives for client to consider—put client in role of expert to evaluate suggestion	1	2	3	4	5
10. Encouragement for student and parent/teacher built in	1	2	3	4	5
11. Commitment to implement plan obtained	1	2	3	4	5
12. Follow-up meeting/phone conference set	1	2	3	4	5

I liked: (strengths of consultation)

Something you may want to consider for next time:

Table D.2   Feedback to Workshop Facilitators

Title of workshop: _____

Name of workshop facilitator: _____

Person providing feedback: _____

Please provide the following information with regard to your experience.

Warm-Up
The "warm-up" helped me get into the topic and got me ready to get involved.

Example/Comments:

Ask before Telling
I was asked to share some of my own ideas before information was presented.

Example/Comments:

Personalize and Practice
As information was shared, I was asked to think about, write, or share some of my own experiences as related to the topic at hand. I was given an opportunity to practice what I was learning.

Example/Comments:

Process and Summarize
At the end of the session, I was asked to reflect on my involvement in the workshop and how I will use what I have learned or relearned.

Example/Comments:

Evaluate
I was asked for feedback about the effectiveness of the workshop in reaching targeted outcomes.

Example/Comments:

The most effective workshop strategy I experienced today was:

Something I might suggest for next time:

COACH

Using the *Peer Coaching Model for Feedback* (Brigman & Campbell, 2002) is encouraged to support and speed skill development. Peer coaching not only helps the school counselor evaluate skill development but also allows the participants to identify particularly effective strategies while strengthening their own learning process. The peer coaching model has been found to be very useful in providing feedback that allows for self-reflection and input from others while maintaining a positive focus.

The following steps are used to facilitate the peer coaching process after a demonstration of the case consultation model or a workshop presentation:

1. One of the participants, not the school counselor who led the workshop or demonstration of case consultation, will facilitate the process that begins by giving participants a few moments to complete their notes and ratings and for the presenter to be thinking about what he or she was able to do that was helpful, useful, and/or particularly effective.
2. The workshop/demonstration presenter is then asked by the facilitator to share what he or she thought was done effectively. It is important for the facilitator to stop the presenter if negatives are mentioned at this point.
3. The presenter is asked if he or she would like to hear other effective skills that were noticed by participants. Participants share what they have noted on their written feedback sheet.
4. Next, the presenter shares what could be done differently next time to make the workshop or consultation even better. After sharing these proposed changes, the presenter is asked if he or she would like to hear suggestions from others.
5. Participants share their suggestions. After giving suggested changes each group member concludes with a positive comment about the experience.
6. Group members give their written feedback sheets to the workshop presenter.

CASE CONSULTATION WITH PARENTS/TEACHERS: BUILDING YOUR SKILLS

Emphasis is placed on building the skills needed to engage in effective consultative experiences with parents and teachers. After receiving an overview of the model and observing specific skill demonstrations, school counselors are given the opportunity to practice their new consultation skills in triads. One person in each group plays the role of the consultant, another plays the role of parent or teacher, and the third person is the observer. Each triad member has the chance to play all roles.

After each practice consultation, feedback is provided using the "Peer Coaching" model. The observer facilitates the feedback process. Tasks to be taught, demonstrated, and practiced are found on the Case Consultation Feedback Form (see Table D.1) and include:

Before the Consultation

- Setting up and preparing for the consultation

During the Consultation

- Structuring the meeting
- Developing the relationship
- Identifying strengths and potential strengths
- Clarifying behaviors
- Making goals specific
- Identifying interventions
- Developing plans for improvement and follow-up

After the Consultation

- Follow-up of consultation

WORKSHOP PRESENTATION

Each school counselor develops a workshop that demonstrates knowledge of a specific content area to include extent of the problem, behaviors that impact school success, strategies that might be shared with teachers and parents, recommended resources, as well as knowledge of workshop development. The workshop presenter provides a workshop outline (following the format provided in Chapter 6) and copies of any handouts or activities used to facilitate the workshop experience to each class member. Background information, resources for parents and teachers, along with this outline provide content as well as a framework for other school counselors to use to prepare workshops in their own schools.

School counselors develop workshop fliers or brochures to promote their presentation. Participants in teacher education courses who may be interested in one or more of the topics could be invited to attend. This creates a more field-based experience as school counselors are extending their experiences beyond their counselor education peer group. Following the workshop, presenters are provided feedback using the Peer Coaching model and using the Feedback to Workshop Facilitators form (see Table D.2).

Sample Workshop Titles

- Setting students up for success
- Helping students manage test anxiety
- Stress management for teachers
- Family friendly schools
- Bully proofing
- Sexual harassment
- Building safe and friendly schools
- Helping students have a successful transition
- Conflict management
- Creating a caring, supportive, and encouraging classroom community
- Motivating low achieving students
- Strategies for helping ADHD students learn
- Using classroom meetings to support a positive climate
- Cognitive skills to improve student learning
- Brain-friendly activities that promote learning and cooperation.

ADDITIONAL ACTIVITIES TO SUPPORT THE TEXT

In addition to case consultation and workshop practice and feedback activities, the following activities provide additional opportunities to build a knowledge base and develop the skills needed for competent consultation: (1) three-part resource collection that supplements the counseling student's workshop topic and (2) school-based observation of a school counselor facilitating a team of professionals.

THREE-PART RESOURCE COLLECTION TO SUPPLEMENT WORKSHOP TOPIC

School counselors develop a resource guide to be shared with peers. The resource collection provides these students the opportunity to increase their familiarity with professional journals and a host of other resources that help to build their knowledge base, making them more effective as counselors and consultants. School counselors develop a paper, resource collection, and book review to support their workshop. This three-part collection (on a single topic) is shared with peers, providing each person with a collection of resources and information on which they can draw as they continue through the program and into their own professional settings. The expectation is that this kind of development and sharing continues as counselors enter their own schools.

See suggested workshop topics in the previous section for focus of Three-Part Collection.

Paper: Building Knowledge and Resources

School counselors select one of the topics frequently addressed through consultation in the schools. A sample five part format for the paper is: (1) describe the extent of the problem, (2) detail the behavioral characteristics frequently exhibited by students (especially those that might impact school success), (3) explain the counselor's role as a consultant working with this issue, (4) provide suggested strategies for teachers/parents working with students exhibiting these behaviors, and (5) reflect on conclusions drawn by the student about his or her ability to be effective working as a consultant in this area.

Resource Collection: Building Knowledge and Resources

School counselors explore and evaluate resources within their chosen topic area. Resources should include professional books or journals, materials available for parents, materials available for teachers, community resources, and Internet sites. Each entry includes a brief annotation as to the intended audience and what the resource might provide. Sources for obtaining the resources should also be included.

Book Review: Building Knowledge and Resources

School counselors review one of the books on their resource list from the popular literature that is meant to be read by parents. This review includes complete bibliographic information, a general synopsis of the book as well as specific contributions—what particular knowledge, insights, skills, or strategies can be gained from reading the book. Reviewers are asked to give examples as well as recommendations for using this book as a resource for parents.

SCHOOL-BASED OBSERVATION: FACILITATING A TEAM OF PROFESSIONALS

School counselors-in-training meet with a school counselor to arrange an opportunity to observe a consultative experience with a team of professionals. Tasks are to notice those strategies/skills that contribute toward the meeting of the consultative goals, to write-up observations, and share the experience with peers. The write-up includes the *purpose/goal(s) of the consultation* (determined prior to the actual consultation), *who was present* (titles only), and *what took place before, during, and after the team meeting that was aimed at reaching the goal(s)*. The *logistics of setting up the consultation as well as follow-through plans* are also noted. School counselors-in-training are asked to notice the *role of the school counselor* in the team meeting process and *how interactions and contributions are facilitated* among the group members. Particular note should be taken of the school counselor's leadership role in the meeting.

The final part of the write-up examines what went well and things they might do differently or strategies they might have included that may have contributed to the effectiveness of the consultation. This is not meant to be evaluative but is a chance for counseling students to demonstrate knowledge of the process and what might have been particularly effective or missing.

SURVEY RESULTS

We have used the activities described in the previous section and found that they have produced consistent results. Recently surveyed students in the school counseling program overwhelmingly agreed or strongly agreed (95% to 100%) with a series of statements reflecting their positive experience using this experiential skill- and knowledge-building approach. The

Table D.3   Self-Assessment of Consultation Knowledge and Skills

Mark the Likert-type scale to indicate where you see yourself with regard to the following knowledge and skills.

	Strongly Disagree	*Disagree*	*Unsure*	*Agree*	*Strongly Agree*
I have knowledge and understanding of the consultative process.	1	2	3	4	5
I have the knowledge and skills to plan and deliver a teacher workshop.	1	2	3	4	5
I have the knowledge and skills to plan and deliver a parent workshop.	1	2	3	4	5
I have the knowledge and skills to facilitate the consultative process with teachers.	1	2	3	4	5
I have the knowledge and skills to facilitate the consultative process with parents.	1	2	3	4	5
I have the knowledge and skills to organize and facilitate team meetings (child study).	1	2	3	4	5
I have knowledge of student behavior (causes and intervention strategies).	1	2	3	4	5
I have started to collect information about resources concerning a wide range of student issues/concerns for use with parents/teachers.	1	2	3	4	5

Continue your assessment by responding to the following:

• I have provided copies of each assignment to all class
   members (hard copy or electronic copy).   Yes   No

• I plan to continue to expand my knowledge base about children/adolescent issues and
   strategies for intervention by: _____
   _____
   _____
   _____

Other comments:

self-assessment (see Table D.3) included rating knowledge and skills in the use of the consultative process with teachers, parents, and administrators; planning and delivering teacher or parent workshops; facilitating team meetings; evaluating knowledge of student behavior and appropriate intervention strategies, as well as building a resource base concerning a wide range of student issues and concerns for use with parents and teachers.

School counselors, as behavior and relationship specialists in their schools, can help others to work more effectively with students through consultation (Myrick, 2003). The models and supporting theories presented in this text, along with the kinds of activities suggested, can be used to deliver an experience that will prepare school counselors for their consultative role.

References

Addiction Technology Transfer Center. (2002). *The change book: A blueprint for technology transfer.* Kansas City: University of Missouri, Addiction Technology Transfer Center.

Adler, A. (1971). *Practice and theory of individual psychology.* New York: Humanitas Press. (Original work published 1927)

Albert, L. (1996). *Cooperative discipline: Classroom management that promotes self-esteem.* Circle Pines, MN: American Guidance Service.

Albert, L. (2003). *Cooperative discipline: Teacher's guide.* Circle Pines, MN: American Guidance Service.

Albert, L., & Einstein, E. (1986). *Strengthening stepfamilies.* Circle Pines, MN: American Guidance Service.

American Counseling Association. (1995). *Ethical standards.* Alexandria, VA: Author.

American School Counselor Association. (2000). *The professional school counselor and critical incident response in the schools.* Alexandria, VA: Author.

American School Counselor Association. (2004). *Ethical standards for school counselors.* Alexandria, VA: Author.

Baker, S. B., & Gerler, E. R., Jr. (2004). *School counseling for the twenty-first century* (4th ed.). Upper Saddle River, NJ: Pearson Education.

Beck, A. T. (1976). *Cognitive therapy and the emotional disorders.* New York: International Universities Press.

Bergan, J. R. (1977). *Behavioral consultation.* Columbus, OH: Merrill.

Bergan, J. R., & Kratochwill, T. R. (1990). *Behavioral consultation and therapy.* New York: Plenum Press.

Bowdoin, R. (1993). *Bowdoin method of parent education II.* Brentwood, TN: Webster's International.

Bowdoin, R. (1996). *Bowdoin method of parent education I.* Brentwood, TN: Webster's International.

Bowers, J., & Hatch, P. (2002). *A national model for school counseling programs.* Alexandria, VA: American School Counseling Association.

Brack, G., Jones, E. S., Smith, R. M., White, J., & Brack, C. J. (1993). A primer on consultation theory: Building a flexible worldview. *Journal of Counseling and Development, 71,* 619–628.

Bradley, F. O. (1997). *Status of school counseling: Structure, governance, and levers for change.* Washington, DC: Education Trust.

Brigman, G. A., & Campbell, C. (2002). *A peer coaching model for school counselors.* Unpublished manuscript.

Brigman, G. A., Campbell, C., & Webb, L. (2004). *Student success skills: Small group counseling manual.* Boca Raton, FL: Atlantic Education Consultants.

Brigman, G. A., Lane, D., & Lane, D. (1994). *Ready to learn.* Minneapolis, MN: Educational Media.

Brigman, G. A., & Webb, L. (2004). *Student success skills: A classroom guidance manual.* Boca Raton, FL: Atlantic Education Consultants.

Browning, L., Davis, B., & Resta, V. (2000). What do you mean "think before I act?" *Journal of Research in Childhood Education, 14,* 232–238.

Campbell, C., & Dahir, C. A. (1997). *The national standards for school counseling programs.* Alexandria, VA: American School Counselor Association.

Caplan, G. (1970). *The theory and practice of mental health consultation.* New York: Basic Books.

Carlson, K. W. (1990). Suggestions for counseling "other"-referred children. *Elementary School Guidance and Counseling, 24,* 222–229.

Committee for Children. (2002). *Second step: A violence prevention curriculum.* Seattle, WA: Committee for Children.

Conoley, J. C., & Conoley, C. W. (1992). *School consultation: Practice and training* (2nd ed.). Boston: Allyn & Bacon.

Council for Accreditation of Counseling and Related Educational Programs. (2001). *CACREP accreditation standards and procedures manual.* Alexandria, VA: Author.

Dahir, C. A., Sheldon, C. B., & Valiga, M. J. (1998). *Vision into action: Implementing the National Standard for School Counseling Programs.* Alexandria, VA: American School Counselor Association.

Deck, M. D. (1992). Training school counselors to be consultants. *Elementary School Guidance and Counseling, 26,* 221–228.

de Shazer, S. (1988). *Clues: Investigating solutions in brief therapy.* New York: Norton.

Dinkmeyer, D. C., & Caldwell, E. (1970). *Developmental counseling and guidance: A comprehensive school approach.* New York: McGraw-Hill.

Dinkmeyer, D. C., & Carlson, J. (1973). *Consulting: Facilitating human potential and change process.* Columbus, OH: Merrill.

Dinkmeyer, D. C., Carlson, J., & Dinkmeyer, D. C., Jr. (2000). *Consultation: Schools mental health professionals as consultants* (2nd ed.). Philadelphia: Brunner/Mazel.

Dinkmeyer, D. C., Dinkmeyer, D. C., Jr., & Sperry, L. (1987). *Adlerian counseling and psychotherapy* (2nd ed.). Columbus, OH: Merrill.

Dinkmeyer, D. C., & Losoncy, L. E. (1992). *The encouragement book.* New York: Simon & Schuster.

Dinkmeyer, D. C., & McKay, G. D. (1982). *Raising a responsible child.* New York: Simon & Schuster.

Dinkmeyer, D. C., & McKay, G. D. (1997a). *STEP* (Systematic Training for Effective Parenting). Circle Pines, MN: American Guidance Service.

Dinkmeyer, D. C., & McKay, G. D. (1997b). *STEP/TEEN* (Systematic Training for Effective Parenting of Teens). Circle Pines, MN: American Guidance Service.

Dinkmeyer, D. C., McKay, G. D., & Dinkmeyer, D. C., Jr. (1980). *STET: Systematic training for effective teaching.* Circle Pines, MN: American Guidance Service.

Dinkmeyer, D. C., McKay, G. D., & Dinkmeyer, D. C., Jr., Dinkmeyer, J. S., & McKay, J. L. (1997). *The next STEP* (Effective parenting through problem-solving). Circle Pines, MN: American Guidance Service.

Dinkmeyer, D. C., McKay, G. D., & Dinkmeyer, J. S. (1997). *Early childhood STEP* (Systematic training for effective parenting of children under six). Circle Pines, MN: American Guidance Service.

Dinkmeyer, D. C., Pew, W. L., & Dinkmeyer, D. C., Jr. (1979). *Adlerian counseling and psychotherapy.* Monterey, CA: Brooks/Cole.

Dougherty, A. M. (2000). *Psychological consultation and collaboration in school and community settings* (3rd ed.). Belmont, CA: Brooks/Cole.

Dougherty, A. M., Dougherty, L. P., & Purcell, D. (1991). The sources and management of resistance to consultation. *School Counselor, 38,* 178–186.

Dougherty, M. (1980). Designing classroom meetings for the middle school child. *School Counselor, 28,* 127–132.

Dreikurs, R., & Grey, L. (1968). *Logical consequences.* New York: Meredith.

Dreikurs, R., & Grey, L. (1970). *A parent's guide to child discipline.* New York: Hawthorn Books.

Dreikurs, R., Grunwald, B. B., & Pepper, F. C. (1998). *Maintaining sanity in the classroom: Illustrated teaching techniques* (2nd ed.). New York: Harper & Row.

Dreikurs, R., & Soltz, V. (1964). *Children: The challenge.* New York: Hawthorn.

Dustin, D., & Ehly, S. (1992). School consultation in the 1990's. *Elementary School Guidance and Counseling, 26,* 165–175.

Edwards, D., & Mullis, F. (2003). Classroom meetings: Encouraging a climate of cooperation. *Professional School Counseling, 7,* 20–28.

Erchul, W. P., & Conoley, C. W. (1991). Helpful theories to guide counselor's practice of school based consultation. *Elementary School Guidance and Counseling, 25,* 204–211.

Fall, M. (1995). Planning for consultation: An aid for the elementary school counselor. *School Counselor, 43,* 151–156.

Faust, V. (1968). *The counselor-consultant in the elementary school.* Boston: Houghton Mifflin.

Gibbs, J. (2001). *Tribes: A new way of learning and being together.* Windsor, CA: CenterSource Systems.

Gilbert, J. (1986). Logical consequences: A new classification. *Individual Psychology, 42,* 243–254.

Gilbert, J. (1989). Logical consequences: A new classification for the classroom. *Individual Psychology, 45,* 425–432.

Glasser, W. (1969). *Schools without failure.* New York: Harper & Row.

Glasser, W. (2000). *Reality therapy in action.* New York: HarperCollins.

Glosoff, H., & Koprowicz, C. (1990). *Children achieving potential: An introduction to elementary school counseling and state-level policies.* Washington, DC: National Conference of State Legislatures and American Association for Counseling and Development.

Gysbers, N. C., & Henderson, P. (2000). *Developing and managing your school guidance program* (3rd ed.). Alexandria, VA: American Counseling Association.

Hattie, J., Biggs, J., & Purdie, N. (1996). Effects of learning skills interventions on student learning: A meta-analysis. *Review of Educational Research, 66*(2), 99–130.

Herring, R. D. (1997). *Multicultural counseling in schools: A synergistic approach.* Alexandria, VA: American Counseling Association.

Idol, L., Nevin, A., & Paolucci-Witcomb, P. (1994). *Collaborative consultation* (2nd ed.). Austin, TX: ProEd.

Keat, D. B. (1990). *Child multimodal therapy.* Norwood, NJ: Ablex.

Kern, R. M., & Mullis, F. (1993). An Adlerian consultation model. *Individual Psychology, 49*(2), 242–247.

Keys, S. G., Bemak, F., Carpenter, S. L., & King-Sears, M. E. (1998). Collaborative consultant: A new role for counselors serving at-risk youths. *Journal of Counseling and Development, 76,* 123–133.

Kottman, T., & Wilborn, B. L. (1992). Parents helping parents: Multiplying the counselor's effectiveness. *School Counselor, 40,* 10–14.

Kratochwill, T. R., & Bergan, J. R. (1990). *Behavioral consultation and theory.* Columbus, OH: Merrill.

Kratochwill, T. R., Sladeezek, L., & Plunge, M. (1995). The evolution of behavioral consultation. *Journal of Educational and Psychological Consultation, 6*(2), 145–157.

Kreidler, W. (1994). *Conflict resolution in the middle school.* Cambridge, MA: Educators for Social Responsibility.

Lazarus, A. (1981). *The practice of multimodal therapy.* New York: McGraw-Hill.

Lewis, B., Schaps, E., & Watson, M. (1996). The caring classroom's academic edge. *Educational Leadership, 54,* 16–21.

Masten, A. S., & Coatsworth, J. D. (1998). The development of competence in favorable and unfavorable environments: Lessons from research on successful children. *American Psychologist, 53*(2), 205–220.

Matthes, W. A., & Dustin, D. (1980). The counselor as trainer: Principles of workshop design. *School Counselor, 27,* 310–313.

Meyers, B., Dowdy, J., & Paterson, P. (2000). Finding the missing voices: Perspectives of the least visible families and their willingness and capacity for school involvement. *Middle Level Education, 7*(2), 59–79.

Mullis, F., & Edwards, D. (2001). Consulting with parents: Applying family systems concepts and techniques. *Professional School Counseling, 5,* 116–123.

Myrick, R. D. (2003). *Developmental guidance and counseling: A practical approach* (4th ed.). Minneapolis, MN: Educational Media.

National PTA. (2000). *Building successful partnerships: A guide for developing parent and family involvement programs.* Bloomington, IN: National Education Service.

Nelsen, J. (1996). *Positive discipline* (2nd ed.). New York: Ballantine Books.

Nelsen, J., Lott, L., & Glenn, H. (1993). *Positive discipline in the classroom: A teacher's guide to classroom meetings.* New York: Ballantine Books.

Nikelly, A. G. (Ed.). (1971). *Techniques for behavior change.* Springfield, IL: Charles C. Thomas.

Omizo, M. M., & Cubberly, W. E. (1983). The effects of reality therapy classroom meetings on self-concept and locus of control among learning disabled students. *Exceptional Child, 30,* 201–209.

Otwell, P. S., & Mullis, F. (1997). Counselor-led staff development: An efficient approach to teacher consultation. *Professional School Counseling, 1*(1), 25–30.

Paisley, P. O., & McMahon, H. G. (2001). School counseling for the 21st century: Challenges and opportunities. *Professional School Counseling, 5*(2), 106–115.

Perusse, R., Goodnough, G. E., & Noel, C. J. (2001). A national survey of school counselor preparation programs: Screening methods, faculty experiences, curricular content, and fieldwork requirements. *Counselor Education and Supervision, 40,* 252–263.

Poland, S., & McCormick, J. (1999). *Coping with a crisis: Lessons learned* (A resource for schools, parents, and communities). Longmont, CO: Sopris West.

Popkin, M. H. (1998a). *Active parenting of teens.* Marietta, GA: Active Parenting.

Popkin, M. H. (1998b). *Family talk.* Marietta, GA: Active Parenting.

Popkin, M. H. (2002). *Active parenting now.* Marietta, GA: Active Parenting.

Rich, D. (1992). *MegaSkills.* Boston: Houghton Mifflin.

178 REFERENCES

Schmidt, F., & Friedman, A. (1990). *Fighting fair.* Miami Beach, FL: Grace Con-
trino Abrams Peace Education Foundation.
Smith, K. (2003, November/December). Turning a crisis into a team. *ASCA
School Counselor, 41,* 13–15.
Sorsdahl, S. N., & Sanche, R. P. (1985). The effects of classroom meetings on
self-concept and behavior. *Elementary School Guidance and Counseling, 20,*
49–56.
Sue, D. W., & Sue, D. (2003). *Counseling the culturally diverse: Theory and prac-
tice* (4th ed.). Hoboken, NJ: Wiley.
United States Department of Education. (2003). *Digest of education statistics,
2002.* Washington, DC: National Center for Education Statistics.
Wang, M. C., Haertel, G. D., & Walberg, H. J. (1994). What helps students learn?
Educational Leadership, 51, 74–79.
Watts, V., & Thomas, B. (1998). *Critical heartbeats: Counselors on the front line.*
Lawrenceville, GA: Gwinnett County Public Schools.
Webb, L. D. (2004). *Keys to school wide discipline: A framework for planning.*
Manuscript in progress.
West, J. F., & Idol, L. (1987). School consultation: An interdisciplinary perspec-
tive on theory, models, and research. *Journal of Learning Disabilities, 20*(7),
388–404.
West, J. F., & Idol, L. (1993). The counselor as consultant in the collaborative
school. *Journal of Counseling and Development, 71,* 678–683.
White, J., & Mullis, F. (1998). A systems approach to school consultation. *Edu-
cation, 119*(2), 242–252.
White, J., Mullis, F., Earley, B., & Brigman, G. (1995). *Consultation in the
schools: The counselor's role.* Portland, ME: J. Weston Walch.
White, J., & Riordan, R. (1990). Some key concerns in leading parent education
groups. *Journal for Specialists in Group Work, 4,* 201–205.
Wilmes, D. J. (2000). *Roots & wings: Raising resilient children.* Center City, MN:
Hazelden.
Wittmer, J. (2000). *Managing your school counseling program: K-12 developmental
strategies* (2nd ed.). Minneapolis, MN: Educational Media.
Wrenn, C. G. (1962). *Counseling in a changing world.* Washington, DC: American
Personnel and Guidance Association Press.

Annotated Bibliography

♦

CONSULTATION

Brown, D., Kurpius, D. J., & Morris, J. R. (1990). *Handbook of consultation with individuals and small groups.* Alexandria, VA: American Association for Counseling and Development.

This handbook provides an overview of consultation in general. The chapter on developing the consultation relationship is of specific interest to the school counselor, as are other sections pertaining to resistance to consultation and ways to evaluate consultation.

Dinkmeyer, D., Carlson, J., & Dinkmeyer, D., Sr. (2000). *Consultation: School mental health professionals as consultants* (2nd ed.). Philadelphia: Brunner/Mazel.

An excellent book based on Adlerian psychology for school counselors who consult with parents, teachers, and administrators. The book is grounded in theory, but offers specific techniques for consulting with individuals, teacher and parent groups, and for working with groups of students in developmental classroom consultation. Case studies are also provided.

Gerler, E. R., Jr. (Ed.). (1992). Consultation and school counseling [Special issue]. *Elementary School Guidance and Counseling, 26*(3).

Must reading for school counselors. This issue contains articles about school consultation in general as well as articles about specific consultation topics for both students and teachers. Ethical concerns and training issues are also addressed.

ETHICS

Corey, G., Corey, M. S., & Callahan, P. (2003). *Issues and ethics in the helping professions* (6th ed.). Pacific Grove, CA: Brooks/Cole.

A frequently used textbook for counseling students. This book discusses ethical issues in the areas of training and supervision; client rights, including confidentiality and duty to warn and protect; and the client/therapist relationship. Ethical concerns in multicultural counseling, marital and family therapy, and in group work are also addressed. What separates this book from other texts on ethical principles is its emphasis on the counselor's personal values and how they relate to ethical practice. Each chapter begins with a self inventory that helps readers assess their own beliefs. The book provides many opportunities for the reader to decide on personal courses of action.

Fischer, L., & Sorenson, G. P. (1996). *School law for counselors, psychologists, and social workers* (3rd ed.). New York: Longman.

This is a good reference book for school counselors. Specific court cases (and how they affect school counselors and other school personnel) are provided in the areas of liability, education records, student discipline, child abuse and neglect, and general rights related to schooling.

Herlihy, B., & Corey, G. (1996). *ACA ethical standards casebook* (5th ed.). Alexandria, VA: American Counseling Association.

This book helps counselors interpret the ACA ethical standards. Although a few situations are relevant for school counselors, most dilemmas are written for professional counselors in general.

Remley, T. P., Hermann, M. K., & Huey, W. C. (2003). *Ethical and legal issues in school counseling* (2nd ed.). Alexandria, VA: American School Counselor Association.

This book contains informative articles from journals that discuss current as well as controversial ethical issues. It begins with a discussion of ethical guidelines and provides an added perspective to ethical challenges. A good reference book.

ADLERIAN THEORY

Bettner, B. L., & Lew, A. (1992). *Raising kids who can.* New York: Harper Perennial.

This little book tells how to use family meetings to nurture responsible, cooperative, caring, and happy children. It discusses getting started, planning agendas, problem solving, and other useful parenting topics.

Dinkmeyer, D., Dinkmeyer, D., Jr., & Sperry, L. (1987). *Adlerian counseling and psychotherapy* (2nd ed.). Columbus, OH: Merrill.

An introductory textbook for students of Adlerian psychology. Several chapters cover the foundations of Adlerian theory, such as the development of the personality and lifestyle, psychopathology, theories of counseling, and counseling techniques. Other chapters provide information about counseling with specific populations, such as children and adolescents, the elderly, and health care counseling. Adlerian counseling methods with groups, family, and the marital couple are also included, as are the use of Adlerian techniques with parent and teachers. A lifestyle guide for use with children is also provided.

Dinkmeyer, D., & Dreikurs, R. (2000). *Encouraging children to learn.* New York: Bruner-Routledge.

Redirecting behavior toward the useful side of life requires the use of encouragement. This book describes basic Adlerian assumptions about the development of personality, discouragement, principles of encouragement, and specific applications of encouragement techniques. Numerous examples of the use of encouragement are given.

Dinkmeyer, D., & Losoncy, L. E. (1992). *The encouragement book.* New York: Simon & Schuster.

A self-help book about encouragement with exercises that could be used or adapted for use with parent and teacher groups or with students. The first part of the book provides knowledge about encouragement and invites readers to examine their attitude about this concept. Part Two focuses on encouragement skills in relationships and communication, and part three helps readers find ways to comfortably use encouragement techniques in their daily life.

Dinkmeyer, D., & McKay, G. D. (1982). *Raising a responsible child.* New York: Simon & Schuster.

A very useful book for educating parents about children's behavior, ways to promote emotional growth, effective communication techniques, encouragement, and promoting responsibility by using consequences rather than punishment. Also included are chapters on dealing with school problems and making family meetings part of the family routine. An interesting chapter discusses "games children play."

Dreikurs, R. (1964). *Children: The challenge.* New York: Hawthorn Books.

This book was used in hundreds of parent study groups before the advent of video-based parenting programs, and it is still very relevant for parents. Understanding the child, goals of misbehavior, and the use of consequences and encouragement are discussed, as are specific recommmendations for handling common parenting concerns, such as sibling conflict, dealing with children's fears, stimulating independence, and dealing with television.

Dreikurs, R. (1972). *Coping with children's misbehavior: A parent's guide.* New York: Hawthorn Books.

This book provides a very thorough discussion of each of the goals of misbehavior. Examples of behaviors typically observed within each of the four goals are given, as are techniques that parents can use to redirect the misbehavior. Nine comprehensive case illustrations are also provided.

Dreikurs, R. (1989). *Fundamentals of Adlerian psychology.* Chicago: School of Professional Psychology.

A brief introduction to some of the major concepts in Adlerian psychology is provided in this short book. Some of the concepts discussed are social interest, the inferiority feeling and striving for significance, heredity and equipment, the lifestyle, crime and insanity, and the three life tasks of work, love, and friendship.

Dreikurs, R., Cassel, P., & Kehoe, D. (1990). *Discipline without tears* (reprint ed.). New York: Dutton.

A very helpful book for teachers (especially at the elementary level). The first chapter helps readers identify their teaching style: autocratic, permissive, or democratic. Other chapters describe the goals of misbehavior, the effects of competition and encouragement on children, the use of logical consequences in the classroom, conflict resolution, classroom discussion groups, and typical problems and how to solve them.

Dreikurs, R., & Grey, L. (1970). *A parents' guide to child discipline.* New York: Hawthorn Books.

Another helpful book for parents. The family constellation, goals of misbehavior, encouragement, and logical consequences are discussed.

Examples of using logical consequences for specific situations, such as fighting, forgetfulness, care of pets, and bedwetting, are provided.

Dreikurs, R., & Grey, L. (1993). *A new approach to discipline: Logical consequences.* New York: Plume.

A comprehensive treatment of the rationale and principles for using logical consequences instead of punishment. Many practical examples of logical consequences that can be used in home and elementary school situations are included, as are examples of using logical consequences with adolescents.

Dreikurs, R., Grunwald, B. B., & Pepper, F. C. (1998). *Maintaining sanity in the classroom* (2nd ed.). Washington, DC: Accelerated Development.

A very useful book. In-depth explanations of children's misbehavior and ways to redirect useless behavior are provided. The uses of encouragement, consequences, and group discussion are discussed in detail, and many examples illustrate the concepts.

Ferguson, E. D. (1995). *Adlerian theory: An introduction.* Chicago: Adler School of Professional Psychology.

A very useful booklet that provides brief explanations of several Adlerian concepts, including social interest, courage, private logic and common sense, family constellation, the psychology of use, emotions, and natural and logical consequences.

Manaster, G. J., & Corsini, R. J. (1993). *Individual psychology: Theory and practice.* Chicago: Adler School of Professional Psychology.

An introductory textbook for students of Adlerian psychology, this book provides definitions of Adlerian terms, discusses personality types and their development and maintenance, and provides an overview of the theory and process of counseling. Also included are chapters on family and group counseling and on education.

Nelsen, J. (1996). *Positive discipline* (2nd ed.). New York: Ballantine Books.

A practical, step-by-step resource book for both parents and teachers. This book not only explains a theory that helps adults understand children, but it also provides practical techniques to help children learn self-discipline, responsibility, problem-solving skills, and cooperation. It includes chapters on birth order, mistaken goals of behavior, natural and logical consequences, and encouragement and contains appendices that tell how to set up peer-counseling groups and parent study groups. Sample invitations, form letters, and brief lesson plans for these groups are also provided.

Walton, F. X. (1980). *Winning teenagers over in home and school.* Columbia, SC: Adlerian Child Care Books.

Another useful booklet for both parents and teachers. The focus of this booklet is on teenagers and the ways adults at home and at school can encourage cooperation and responsible behavior. The problems engendered by pampering and coerciveness are discussed, as are more useful ways of dealing with teens. Specific tips are provided for teachers to use when dealing with each of the mistaken goals of behavior.

Walton, F. X., & Powers, R. L. (1974). *Winning children over: A manual for teachers, counselors, principals, and parents.* Chicago: Practical Psychology Associates.

A brief introduction to understanding children's goals of misbehavior, helping children change, and working with the class as a group. Also included are ways to develop cooperation and responsibility in children. A very useful resource booklet to keep on your shelf for parents and teachers.

◆ *Author Index*

◆ Subject Index

Greg Brigman, PhD, is a professor in the Department of Counselor Education at Florida Atlantic University. He is a former high school teacher, school counselor, and has worked with students from elementary to high school. Dr. Brigman is the coordinator of the school counselor program at FAU and has published in the area of school consultation. He developed a course in school consultation that he teaches regularly at FAU. Dr. Brigman works with school districts to develop effective counseling programs and to evaluate the impact of school counselors on student achievement and behavior. He presents training workshops related to school counseling nationally and internationally and is a regular presenter at professional conferences.

Fran Mullis, PhD, is an associate professor in the Department of Counseling and Psychological Services at Georgia State University where she has been a counselor educator for 15 years. She coordinates the school counseling program and collaborated on the development of a course in School Counselor Consultation that uses the concepts and skills presented in this text. Dr. Mullis has taught the consultation course for a number of years, and she supervises school counselors-in-training who put into practice the consultation skills taught. Dr. Mullis has experience as a school counselor and has published in the area of school counselor consultation and school counseling.

Linda D. Webb, PhD, is an assistant professor in the Department of counselor Education at Florida Atlantic University. She has three years experience as a counselor educator preceded by 17 years experience as a school counselor and guidance director at the elementary and high school levels. Dr. Webb has published and presented on many topics critical to student success. She has worked collaboratively to develop and teach a course in school counselor consultation based on the concepts, skills, and strategies presented in this text.

JoAnna White, EdD, is professor and chair of the Department of Counseling and Psychological Services at Georgia State University. She has 22 years of experience as a counselor educator and 8 years of public school counseling experience. She is published in the area of school counselor consultation. She developed and taught a course in School Counselor Consultation at Georgia State University.

Dana Edwards, PhD, (contributing author) is an associate professor in the Department of Counseling and Psychological Services at Georgia State University. For more than 11 years she has taught courses on school counseling and personality development and socialization. She also has experience as a high school teacher and elementary school counselor. Dr. Edwards is currently involved in research on the efficacy of classroom meetings and program evaluation for school counselors.